SQL FOR DATA ANALYSTS

Transform Raw Data into Insights with SQL

THOMPSON CARTER

TABLE OF CONTENTS

INTRODUCTION

SQL for Data Analysts: Transform Raw Data into Insights with SQL

In today's data-driven world, the ability to harness and analyze data is one of the most valuable skills a professional can possess. Whether you're working in finance, marketing, e-commerce, or any other industry, data analysis plays a pivotal role in making informed decisions and driving business success. Among the myriad tools and languages used for data analysis, **SQL** (Structured Query Language) remains one of the most fundamental and versatile.

This book, **SQL for Data Analysts: Transform Raw Data into Insights with SQL**, is designed to equip you with the necessary skills to turn raw data into actionable insights using SQL—no matter your industry or level of experience. Through this guide, you'll learn not only the basics of SQL, but also how to apply advanced techniques to analyze, clean, and transform data, uncover trends, and generate meaningful reports. This book is jargon-free, providing straightforward, real-world examples that allow you to grasp SQL concepts and immediately apply them in practical scenarios.

Why SQL?

SQL is the cornerstone of relational databases, and relational databases power everything from small businesses to large enterprises. The ubiquity and power of SQL stem from its simplicity and flexibility in managing and querying data. When businesses rely on vast amounts of data—such as sales transactions, customer information, inventory records, or financial data—SQL provides a streamlined way to access, analyze, and manipulate this data quickly and efficiently.

Unlike many programming languages, SQL is specifically designed to query and manipulate relational databases. With SQL, data analysts can:

- Retrieve specific pieces of data from vast datasets.
- Aggregate and summarize data to spot trends and anomalies.
- Filter, sort, and join datasets to answer complex business questions.
- Clean and transform raw data into a usable format for reporting and analysis.
- Create views and reports for stakeholders who need actionable insights.

SQL's importance is compounded by its role as a **universal language** for relational databases. Whether you're working with MySQL, PostgreSQL, Microsoft SQL Server, or any other SQL-based database, the fundamental principles and commands of SQL remain the same. This cross-platform consistency makes SQL a must-have tool in a data analyst's toolbox.

The Goal of This Book

The primary goal of this book is to demystify SQL for data analysts, both beginners and intermediate users. We aim to equip you with practical SQL skills that will allow you to:

1. **Transform raw data into insights**: Learn how to filter, aggregate, join, and analyze data to answer specific business questions. SQL is a powerful tool for cleaning messy data, uncovering trends, and generating actionable insights.

2. **Understand real-world applications**: Each chapter is filled with real-world examples to demonstrate how SQL is used in everyday business scenarios. Whether you're analyzing sales data, customer behavior, or financial trends, you'll walk through examples that mirror common tasks faced by data analysts across industries.

3. **Build a strong foundation**: SQL can be intimidating at first, especially for those new to data analysis. This book starts from the basics and gradually builds up to more complex topics, ensuring you understand the concepts and techniques before diving into advanced applications.

4. **Apply SQL to business decisions**: SQL is a tool for business problem-solving. By the end of this book, you'll not only know how to write SQL queries but also understand how to leverage SQL to make data-driven decisions that benefit your business.

What Will You Learn?

This book is divided into **six parts**, each addressing different aspects of SQL for data analysis. Let's break down what you will learn in each part:

Part 1: Getting Started with SQL for Data Analysis

In this section, you'll begin by understanding what SQL is, why it's essential for data analysis, and how it fits into the broader context of relational databases. We will introduce basic SQL commands (SELECT, FROM, WHERE) and provide a simple, hands-on approach to querying data from tables. By the end of this section, you will be able to retrieve and filter data from a single table.

Part 2: Working with Data in SQL

Now that you're familiar with the basics, we will delve deeper into SQL's data manipulation capabilities. This section covers sorting and limiting data, aggregating results using SQL functions (e.g., COUNT, SUM, AVG), and combining data from multiple tables with **joins**. These techniques are fundamental for performing more advanced data analysis tasks like summarizing sales data, calculating total revenue, or identifying product trends.

Part 3: Advanced SQL Techniques for Data Analysis

Here, we explore advanced SQL features like subqueries, **CASE** statements for conditional logic, and window functions that allow for more sophisticated data analysis. By learning how to rank products, calculate running totals, and apply dynamic filters, you'll be able to answer complex business questions and perform high-level analysis in SQL.

Part 4: Data Transformation and Cleaning with SQL

No data analysis is complete without proper data cleaning. In this section, we focus on how to transform and clean data using SQL. We will cover common tasks like handling NULL values, normalizing and denormalizing data, and making sure your data is in the right format for analysis. You'll also learn how to handle missing data, which is one of the most common challenges when working with real-world datasets.

Part 5: Optimizing and Managing SQL Queries

Efficiency is key when working with large datasets, so this section focuses on optimizing your SQL queries. You'll learn about indexing, query optimization, and how to work with large datasets using techniques like partitioning and batch processing. These skills are invaluable when analyzing big data or running complex queries on enterprise-level databases.

Part 6: Real-World Applications and Case Studies

In this final part, we take everything you've learned and apply it to real-world business scenarios. You'll work through case studies on topics like **financial data analysis**, **customer behavior analysis**, and **sales and marketing analysis**. Each case study will show you how to apply SQL to solve common business problems, such as identifying top customers, analyzing sales trends, and evaluating marketing campaign effectiveness. The book concludes with a final project where you'll use SQL to analyze a retail company's sales data from start to finish.

Who This Book Is For

This book is intended for data analysts of all levels—whether you're just getting started with SQL or you're looking to improve your skills. If you're a beginner, we provide clear explanations and practical examples to help you build confidence with SQL. If you're already familiar with the basics, the book's advanced techniques and real-world case studies will expand your knowledge and equip you with the tools to tackle complex data analysis tasks.

Even if you are an experienced SQL user, this book will provide you with practical, real-world applications of SQL in the context of business analysis. Each chapter is focused on real data and practical examples that you can relate to, allowing you to take your SQL skills to the next level.

The world of data analysis is vast, and SQL is the key that unlocks its potential. By mastering SQL, you gain the ability to work with and derive meaningful insights from data—skills that are highly valued in virtually every industry today. This book will guide you from the basics to advanced techniques, showing you how to apply SQL to solve real-world problems in business.

As you progress through this book, you'll not only learn how to write efficient SQL queries but also how to think critically about data—how to clean it, transform it, analyze it, and most importantly, turn it into insights that can drive decisions and improve business outcomes.

By the end of this journey, you'll be ready to apply SQL to your own datasets, tackle complex analytical challenges, and contribute meaningfully to your organization's data-driven decision-making processes.

CHAPTER 1: INTRODUCTION TO SQL FOR DATA ANALYSTS

What is SQL and Why It Is Essential for Data Analysis?

SQL, which stands for **Structured Query Language**, is a standardized programming language used to manage and manipulate relational databases. For data analysts, SQL is an indispensable tool. It's the most common method for querying, extracting, and analyzing data stored in relational databases. SQL allows analysts to perform critical operations like retrieving data, summarizing information, and transforming raw data into actionable insights. Whether you're working with sales figures, customer data, or product information, SQL enables you to organize and query large datasets efficiently.

In the context of **data analysis**, SQL plays a key role in:

- **Data Extraction**: Retrieving the necessary data from databases to work with.

- **Data Transformation**: Cleaning, aggregating, and transforming data into a form suitable for analysis.

- **Data Aggregation**: Summarizing large volumes of data to uncover trends and patterns.

- **Data Filtering**: Narrowing down data to focus on specific subsets, such as a particular date range or product category.

SQL is designed to handle structured data, which is data organized into rows and columns within tables—just like how data is typically presented in Excel or a CSV file. This makes SQL an ideal tool for relational databases, where data is stored in tables that are connected by relationships.

Brief Overview of Relational Databases and SQL's Role in Querying Data

A **relational database** is a type of database that stores data in a structured format, using rows and columns. Tables in a relational database are related to one another through **keys**, typically a **primary key** and **foreign keys**.

- **Primary Key**: A unique identifier for each record in a table. For example, in a "Customers" table, the customer ID might be the primary key.

- **Foreign Key**: A field in one table that links to the primary key in another table, creating a relationship between the two tables. For example, a "Orders" table might use a customer ID as a foreign key to reference the corresponding customer in the "Customers" table.

SQL's role in querying data from a relational database is to enable analysts to retrieve, manipulate, and interact with the data stored in these tables. The **SELECT** statement is the most commonly used SQL command, allowing you to fetch data from one or more tables. SQL can also be used to perform operations like sorting, filtering, and summarizing data.

The primary components of SQL are:

- **Data Definition Language (DDL)**: Includes commands like CREATE, ALTER, and DROP for defining database structures (tables, indexes, etc.).
- **Data Manipulation Language (DML)**: Includes commands like SELECT, INSERT, UPDATE, and DELETE for querying and modifying data.
- **Data Control Language (DCL)**: Includes commands like GRANT and REVOKE for controlling access to data.
- **Transaction Control Language (TCL)**: Includes commands like COMMIT, ROLLBACK, and SAVEPOINT for managing transactions.

In this chapter, we'll focus primarily on **DML**—specifically the SELECT command and its role in querying and analyzing data.

Understanding Databases, Tables, and the Data Retrieval Process

To effectively use SQL, it's important to first understand the **structure** of relational databases:

- **Database**: A collection of related data stored in a structured format. A database can contain multiple tables, views, and other objects.
- **Table**: A collection of data organized in rows and columns. Each table represents a specific entity or concept (e.g., Customers, Orders, Products).
- **Column**: A field in a table that contains specific types of data (e.g., Customer Name, Product Price).
- **Row**: A record in the table, where each row contains data for a specific instance of the entity (e.g., a specific customer or order).

When performing data analysis, you'll typically retrieve data by writing **SQL queries** that target specific tables, columns, and rows. A query can include a variety of commands and clauses to filter, aggregate, and join data across multiple tables. SQL helps transform raw data into insights by allowing analysts to:

1. **Select specific columns** of data.

2. **Filter** data based on conditions (e.g., only sales from the last quarter).

3. **Aggregate** data to calculate summaries (e.g., total sales, average price).

4. **Join multiple tables** to combine information from different sources (e.g., joining sales with customer data).

Real-World Example: Exploring a Retail Database to Understand Sales Data

Let's walk through a simple example of how SQL can be used to explore a **retail database**. Imagine we have a database that contains the following tables:

- **Customers**: Information about each customer (ID, Name, Email, etc.).

- **Products**: Details about the products sold (Product ID, Name, Category, Price, etc.).

- **Sales**: Information about each sale (Sale ID, Customer ID, Product ID, Quantity Sold, Sale Date, Total Sale Value, etc.).

Step 1: Retrieving Basic Data

First, we want to get a sense of the data. We can use a simple SELECT query to retrieve the top few rows from the **Sales** table.

sql

SELECT * FROM Sales LIMIT 5;

This query retrieves all columns from the **Sales** table and limits the result to the first 5 rows. We can quickly see what each sale record looks like.

Step 2: Analyzing Sales by Product

Next, let's say we want to analyze how much revenue each product generated. To do this, we can use the SUM function to aggregate the **Total Sale Value** by **Product ID**.

sql

SELECT ProductID, SUM(TotalSaleValue) AS Revenue
FROM Sales
GROUP BY ProductID
ORDER BY Revenue DESC;

This query groups the sales by **ProductID**, calculates the total revenue for each product, and orders the results in descending order of revenue.

Step 3: Joining Tables to Analyze Sales by Customer

To gain more insight into who is purchasing the products, we can join the **Sales** table with the **Customers** table. This will allow us to retrieve customer names along with their total purchase amount.

sql

```
SELECT    Customers.Name,    SUM(Sales.TotalSaleValue)    AS
TotalSpent
FROM Sales
JOIN Customers ON Sales.CustomerID = Customers.CustomerID
GROUP BY Customers.Name
ORDER BY TotalSpent DESC;
```

This query retrieves the customer names and the total amount they've spent on purchases, ordered from the highest to the lowest spender.

Step 4: Filtering Sales by Date Range

Let's say we want to focus on sales that occurred in the last quarter. We can filter the **Sales** table using a WHERE clause to limit the date range.

sql

```
SELECT ProductID, SUM(TotalSaleValue) AS Revenue
FROM Sales
WHERE SaleDate BETWEEN '2023-07-01' AND '2023-09-30'
GROUP BY ProductID
ORDER BY Revenue DESC;
```

This query filters sales to only those that occurred between July 1st and September 30th, 2023, and then aggregates the data by **ProductID**.

In this chapter, we've covered the following key points:

- **SQL is essential for data analysis**, enabling analysts to query, transform, and summarize data stored in relational databases.
- **Relational databases** organize data into tables, where each table consists of rows (records) and columns (fields).
- SQL is the primary tool for retrieving and manipulating this data, with the **SELECT** statement being the cornerstone of most SQL queries.
- We explored **real-world examples**, including retrieving sales data, aggregating revenue by product, joining data from different tables, and filtering sales by date.

In the next chapter, we will dive deeper into **setting up your SQL environment** and walk through the practical steps of using SQL tools and interfaces to begin your data analysis journey.

CHAPTER 2: SETTING UP YOUR SQL ENVIRONMENT

Installing SQL-Based Tools (e.g., MySQL, PostgreSQL, SQLite) and Setting Up a Local or Cloud Database

To get started with SQL, you need to install the necessary tools that allow you to interact with relational databases. There are several SQL-based database management systems (DBMS) you can choose from. Each system has its own strengths and use cases, but all are capable of running SQL queries to manage and analyze your data.

1. Installing MySQL: MySQL is one of the most popular relational database systems. It's known for its simplicity and scalability, making it a great choice for both small applications and large enterprises.

- **Step 1**: Download the MySQL installer from the <u>official website</u>.
- **Step 2**: Run the installer and choose the "Developer Default" setup type, which includes the MySQL server and essential tools.
- **Step 3**: During installation, set a root password for MySQL. This password will be used to authenticate your connection.
- **Step 4**: Complete the installation and verify by running the following command in your terminal:

bash

mysql -u root -p

Enter the root password, and you should be connected to the MySQL server.

2. Installing PostgreSQL: PostgreSQL is another powerful, open-source relational database system. It's often chosen for its advanced features and compliance with SQL standards.

- **Step 1**: Download the PostgreSQL installer from the <u>official website</u>.
- **Step 2**: Run the installer and follow the setup prompts. Choose your installation directory, set a password for the PostgreSQL superuser (called postgres), and remember this password for later.

- **Step 3**: Complete the installation and verify by running the following command in the terminal:

bash

psql -U postgres

Enter the postgres password to connect to the PostgreSQL database.

3. Installing SQLite: SQLite is a lightweight, serverless SQL database engine. It's ideal for smaller projects and when you need a portable database that doesn't require a dedicated server.

- **Step 1**: SQLite doesn't require a complex installation process. You can download the command-line tools from the official website.
- **Step 2**: After downloading, extract the files and place them in a directory included in your system's PATH variable for easy access from the command line.
- **Step 3**: To verify your installation, run:

bash

sqlite3

You'll enter the SQLite command-line interface, where you can begin creating and interacting with databases.

Introduction to SQL Query Editors and Management Tools

Once you have your database system installed, you need a **query editor** or **management tool** to interact with your database. These tools provide a graphical interface that makes writing and executing SQL queries much easier. Below are some commonly used tools:

1. MySQL Workbench (for MySQL): MySQL Workbench is an official, cross-platform tool that helps you manage MySQL databases. It provides an easy-to-use interface to create databases, design tables, and write SQL queries.

- **Key Features:**
    - Visual design tools for creating and managing database schemas.
    - Query editor for running and testing SQL queries.
    - Data modeling and ER diagram tools to visualize relationships between tables.
- **How to Use**:

1. After installation, launch MySQL Workbench.
    2. Create a new connection using the root user and the password you set during installation.
    3. Start writing SQL queries in the **SQL Editor** tab.

2. pgAdmin (for PostgreSQL): pgAdmin is the official management tool for PostgreSQL. It provides a comprehensive interface for managing PostgreSQL databases and running queries.

- **Key Features:**
  - o SQL Query Tool for executing SQL statements.
  - o Graphical interface to create and modify databases, tables, and views.
  - o Support for managing large datasets and PostgreSQL extensions.
- **How to Use**:

1. After installation, launch pgAdmin.
   2. Create a new connection to your PostgreSQL server using the postgres user and the password you set.
   3. Write SQL queries in the **Query Tool**.

3. DataGrip (Cross-Platform, for Multiple DBMS): DataGrip is a powerful SQL IDE from JetBrains that supports multiple database systems, including MySQL, PostgreSQL, SQLite, and many others. It's a versatile tool for professional developers and analysts.

- **Key Features:**
  - o Supports a wide range of DBMS.
  - o Advanced SQL editor with code completion, refactoring tools, and error highlighting.

o Integrated version control for managing SQL scripts.

- **How to Use**:

1.   After installing DataGrip, connect to your database by entering the connection details.

2. Use the **SQL Console** to write and execute queries.

Real-World Example: Setting Up an Environment for Analyzing Company Sales Data

Let's walk through setting up an environment where you'll analyze **sales data** for a fictional company using **MySQL**.

Step 1: Install MySQL Follow the installation steps for MySQL as described above and ensure you have MySQL Workbench installed.

Step 2: Create a Database for Sales Data Once MySQL is set up, open MySQL Workbench and create a new database called CompanySales.

1. Launch MySQL Workbench and log in with your root credentials.

2. In the **Query Editor**, enter the following command to create the database:

sql

CREATE DATABASE CompanySales;

USE CompanySales;

Step 3: Create Tables to Store Sales Data Next, let's define the tables to store sales, customers, and products information.

1. **Customers Table**: This table stores customer information such as their name and contact details.

   sql

   ```
   CREATE TABLE Customers (
     CustomerID INT PRIMARY KEY AUTO_INCREMENT,
     CustomerName VARCHAR(255),
     Email VARCHAR(255),
     Phone VARCHAR(15)
   );
   ```

2. **Products Table**: This table stores product details like product name and price.

   sql

   ```
   CREATE TABLE Products (
     ProductID INT PRIMARY KEY AUTO_INCREMENT,
     ProductName VARCHAR(255),
     Price DECIMAL(10, 2)
   );
   ```

3. **Sales Table**: This table stores the sales transaction details, such as the customer, product sold, quantity, and total sale value.

sql

```
CREATE TABLE Sales (
  SaleID INT PRIMARY KEY AUTO_INCREMENT,
  CustomerID INT,
  ProductID INT,
  Quantity INT,
  SaleDate DATE,
  TotalSaleValue DECIMAL(10, 2),
  FOREIGN KEY (CustomerID) REFERENCES Customers(CustomerID),
  FOREIGN KEY (ProductID) REFERENCES Products(ProductID)
);
```

Step 4: Populate the Tables with Sample Data Now that the tables are created, you can insert sample data to simulate sales transactions.

sql

```
-- Inserting customers
INSERT INTO Customers (CustomerName, Email, Phone)
```

VALUES

('John Doe', 'johndoe@example.com', '123-456-7890'),

('Jane Smith', 'janesmith@example.com', '987-654-3210');

-- Inserting products

INSERT INTO Products (ProductName, Price)

VALUES

('Laptop', 1200.50),

('Smartphone', 799.99),

('Headphones', 150.75);

-- Inserting sales transactions

INSERT INTO Sales (CustomerID, ProductID, Quantity, SaleDate, TotalSaleValue)

VALUES

(1, 1, 1, '2023-10-01', 1200.50),

(1, 3, 2, '2023-10-02', 301.50),

(2, 2, 1, '2023-10-03', 799.99);

Step 5: Query and Analyze the Data With the data in place, you can now begin querying the data to analyze sales performance.

For example, to see the total sales value by product:

sql

SELECT Products.ProductName, SUM(Sales.TotalSaleValue) AS
TotalRevenue
FROM Sales
JOIN Products ON Sales.ProductID = Products.ProductID
GROUP BY Products.ProductName;

This query will return the total revenue generated from each product sold, allowing you to analyze product performance.

In this chapter, we covered:

- **Installing SQL-based tools**: We discussed the installation steps for MySQL, PostgreSQL, and SQLite, providing the necessary commands to get started with each.
- **SQL query editors and management tools**: We introduced tools like MySQL Workbench, pgAdmin, and DataGrip that facilitate SQL query writing and database management.
- **Real-world example**: We walked through setting up a local database for analyzing sales data, creating tables for customers, products, and sales, and running simple queries to analyze sales performance.

In the next chapter, we will explore how to **write basic SQL queries** to retrieve and manipulate data in more detail.

CHAPTER 3: BASIC SQL SYNTAX AND QUERIES

Introduction to Basic SQL Syntax (SELECT, FROM, WHERE)

At the heart of SQL is the ability to retrieve and manipulate data stored in relational databases. The basic building blocks of SQL queries are simple commands that allow you to interact with the data efficiently. In this chapter, we'll focus on the foundational syntax of SQL, which is essential for retrieving data and starting your data analysis.

The three most fundamental parts of any SQL query are:

1. **SELECT**: Specifies the columns (fields) you want to retrieve from the database.
2. **FROM**: Specifies the table from which you want to retrieve the data.
3. **WHERE**: Filters the data to return only the rows that meet specific conditions.

These components form the core of most SQL queries, enabling you to retrieve data that is relevant to your analysis.

Basic Syntax Overview:

sql

SELECT column1, column2, ...
FROM table_name
WHERE condition;

- **SELECT**: Here you list the columns you want to return. If you want to select all columns, use * (wildcard).
- **FROM**: This specifies the table from which the data should be retrieved.
- **WHERE**: The condition filters the data. For example, it can limit the rows returned to only those that meet certain criteria, such as a specific customer or product.

Let's break down each of these clauses in more detail.

Writing Simple SELECT Queries to Retrieve Data from a Single Table

1. SELECTing Specific Columns

The simplest query involves retrieving specific columns from a table. For example, if you want to retrieve customer names and their emails from a customer table, you can write a query like this:

sql

```
SELECT CustomerName, Email
FROM Customers;
```

This query retrieves the **CustomerName** and **Email** columns from the **Customers** table. The result will be a list of all customers along with their email addresses.

2. SELECTing All Columns with the Asterisk (*)

If you're interested in retrieving all the columns from a table, you can use the asterisk (*) wildcard. For example:

sql

```
SELECT *
FROM Customers;
```

This query will return every column in the **Customers** table for all rows. While this is convenient, it's generally not recommended for large datasets unless you really need all the data.

3. Filtering Data with WHERE Clause

The **WHERE** clause allows you to filter data based on specific conditions. It is used to specify which rows should be returned based on the values in one or more columns.

For example, if you want to retrieve the customer details of a specific customer, you can use the **WHERE** clause:

sql

```
SELECT CustomerName, Email
FROM Customers
WHERE CustomerID = 1;
```

This query retrieves the **CustomerName** and **Email** of the customer whose **CustomerID** is 1. The WHERE clause limits the results to only those rows where the CustomerID matches the specified value.

Common Operators for WHERE Clause:

- =: Equals. E.g., WHERE Age = 25.
- <> or !=: Not equal. E.g., WHERE Age != 25.
- <, >, <=, >=: Comparison operators for ranges. E.g., WHERE Price > 100.
- **BETWEEN**: To specify a range. E.g., WHERE SaleDate BETWEEN '2023-01-01' AND '2023-12-31'.
- **LIKE**: For pattern matching (e.g., using % as a wildcard). E.g., WHERE Name LIKE 'John%'.
- **IN**: To match any value from a list. E.g., WHERE Country IN ('USA', 'Canada').

For example, retrieving all customers from the **Customers** table whose **CustomerName** starts with "J" would look like this:

sql

```
SELECT CustomerName, Email
FROM Customers
WHERE CustomerName LIKE 'J%';
```

This query retrieves all customers whose names begin with the letter "J" (e.g., "John", "Jane").

Real-World Example: Retrieving Customer Details from an E-Commerce Database

Let's imagine we have an e-commerce database with the following **Customers** table structure:

Customer ID	CustomerN ame	Email	Addre ss	Pho ne	JoinDa te
1	John Doe	johndoe@example. com	123 Elm St	123-456-7890	2021-05-15
2	Jane Smith	janesmith@example .com	456 Oak St	987-654-3210	2020-09-10
3	Bob Brown	bobbrown@exampl e.com	789 Pine St	555-123-4567	2022-01-20

We want to retrieve specific customer details from this table, including their **CustomerName**, **Email**, and **Phone**.

Step 1: Retrieving All Customer Information

To retrieve all the details for every customer, we can use the * wildcard:

sql

```sql
SELECT CustomerName, Email, Phone
FROM Customers;
```

This query will return the **CustomerName**, **Email**, and **Phone** for all customers in the **Customers** table.

Step 2: Retrieving Information for a Specific Customer

Suppose we want to get the details of a customer with **CustomerID = 2**. Using the WHERE clause:

sql

```sql
SELECT CustomerName, Email, Phone
FROM Customers
WHERE CustomerID = 2;
```

This query will only return the **CustomerName**, **Email**, and **Phone** for **Jane Smith**.

Step 3: Filtering Customers Who Joined After a Certain Date

Let's say we want to see all customers who joined after **2021-01-01**. We can use the WHERE clause with the BETWEEN operator:

sql

```sql
SELECT CustomerName, Email, JoinDate
FROM Customers
WHERE JoinDate > '2021-01-01';
```

This query will return customers who joined after January 1st, 2021. The result will include **Jane Smith** and **Bob Brown**, but not **John Doe** since he joined earlier.

Step 4: Retrieving Customers Who Live in a Specific City

Imagine we have an **Address** column, and we want to retrieve customers who live in **"Oak St"**. You can use the LIKE operator to search for partial matches:

sql

```
SELECT CustomerName, Address, Email
FROM Customers
WHERE Address LIKE '%Oak St%';
```

This query will return all customers whose address contains "Oak St," which in this case would return **Jane Smith**.

In this chapter, we've covered the basic syntax of SQL queries, focusing on the three core components:

- **SELECT**: Used to specify the columns to retrieve.
- **FROM**: Specifies the table from which to retrieve data.
- **WHERE**: Filters data based on specific conditions.

We also explored real-world examples using an **e-commerce database**, demonstrating how to write queries to retrieve customer information based on various criteria.

In the next chapter, we will dive deeper into more advanced filtering techniques using **logical operators**, **sorting** results, and **combining multiple conditions** for more complex queries.

CHAPTER 4: FILTERING DATA WITH WHERE CLAUSES

Using Conditions to Filter Data (e.g., WHERE, AND, OR, LIKE, IN, BETWEEN)

The **WHERE** clause is a critical part of any SQL query. It allows you to filter data based on specific conditions, ensuring that only the rows that meet certain criteria are included in the query results. SQL offers a variety of operators and functions that allow you to filter data in ways that are tailored to your needs.

In this chapter, we will explore:

- How to use basic filtering operators like **WHERE, AND, OR, LIKE, IN**, and **BETWEEN**.
- More advanced filtering techniques using **comparison operators** and **logical operators**.

1. Basic Filtering Operators

1.1. The WHERE Clause

The WHERE clause is used to specify the conditions that the rows in the database must meet in order to be included in the query result. For example:

sql

```
SELECT CustomerName, Email
FROM Customers
WHERE CustomerID = 1;
```

This query retrieves the **CustomerName** and **Email** of the customer whose **CustomerID** is 1.

1.2. The AND Operator

The **AND** operator is used when you want to filter data based on multiple conditions. All conditions must be true for a row to be included in the result.

Example: Retrieve customers who live in **"Oak St"** and joined after **2021-01-01**.

sql

```
SELECT CustomerName, Address, JoinDate
FROM Customers
WHERE Address LIKE '%Oak St%' AND JoinDate > '2021-01-01';
```

Here, the query will return only customers who meet both criteria (live on Oak St **and** joined after 2021).

1.3. The OR Operator

The **OR** operator is used when you want to filter data based on multiple conditions, where any of the conditions being true will include the row in the result.

Example: Retrieve customers who either live on **"Oak St"** or **"Elm St"**.

sql

```
SELECT CustomerName, Address
FROM Customers
WHERE Address LIKE '%Oak St%' OR Address LIKE '%Elm St%';
```

This query will return customers who live on either **Oak St** or **Elm St**, even if one condition is true and the other is false.

1.4. The LIKE Operator

The **LIKE** operator is used to search for patterns within text fields. It allows for more flexible matching by using wildcards.

- **%**: Represents zero or more characters.
- **_**: Represents exactly one character.

Example: Retrieve all customers whose names start with "John".

sql

```sql
SELECT CustomerName, Email
FROM Customers
WHERE CustomerName LIKE 'John%';
```

This query will return any customer whose **CustomerName** starts with "John", such as **John Doe**.

1.5. The IN Operator

The **IN** operator allows you to filter data by specifying a list of values. It is more efficient than using multiple OR conditions, especially with larger datasets.

Example: Retrieve customers who are from either **"USA"** or **"Canada"**.

sql

```sql
SELECT CustomerName, Country
FROM Customers
WHERE Country IN ('USA', 'Canada');
```

This query will return customers who are either from the **USA** or **Canada**, regardless of other conditions.

1.6. The BETWEEN Operator

The **BETWEEN** operator is used to filter data by specifying a range of values. It can be applied to numbers, dates, or text.

Example: Retrieve sales data for the **first quarter** of **2023**.

sql

SELECT SaleID, SaleDate, TotalSaleValue
FROM Sales
WHERE SaleDate BETWEEN '2023-01-01' AND '2023-03-31';

This query will return sales transactions that occurred between January 1, 2023, and March 31, 2023.

2. Advanced Filtering with Comparison and Logical Operators

2.1. Comparison Operators

Comparison operators are used in conjunction with the WHERE clause to filter data based on specific comparisons. These include:

- =: Equal to
- <> or !=: Not equal to
- <: Less than
- >: Greater than
- <=: Less than or equal to
- >=: Greater than or equal to

Example: Retrieve products with a price greater than 100:

sql

SELECT ProductName, Price
FROM Products

WHERE Price > 100;

This query returns all products where the price is greater than **100**.

2.2. Combining Logical Operators

You can combine multiple conditions using logical operators like **AND, OR**, and **NOT** to create complex filters.

Example: Retrieve sales transactions where the **TotalSaleValue** is greater than **500**, and the sale date is within the first half of **2023**:

sql

```
SELECT SaleID, SaleDate, TotalSaleValue
FROM Sales
WHERE TotalSaleValue > 500 AND SaleDate BETWEEN '2023-01-01' AND '2023-06-30';
```

This query filters sales where the total sale value is more than **500** and the transaction happened between January 1st and June 30th, 2023.

2.3. Using NOT for Exclusions

The **NOT** operator negates a condition, so it returns rows where the condition is false.

Example: Retrieve customers who **did not** join in 2023:

sql

```
SELECT CustomerName, JoinDate
FROM Customers
WHERE NOT JoinDate BETWEEN '2023-01-01' AND '2023-12-31';
```

This query retrieves customers who did **not** join in **2023**.

3. Real-World Example: Analyzing Sales Transactions Based on Date Ranges and Product Categories

In this example, we will analyze sales transactions from a **sales database** that includes **Products** and **Sales** tables. We want to answer the following questions:

1. What were the total sales for products in the **"Electronics"** category in **2023**?
2. Which sales transactions occurred between **March 1st and March 15th**, 2023, for products priced **above $100**?

Example Table Structure:

Sales.SaleID	Sales.CustomerID	Sales.ProductID	Sales.SaleDate	Sales.Quantity	Sales.TotalSaleValue
1	1	2	2023-03-05	2	1599.98
2	2	3	2023-03-	1	750.00

Sales.SaleID	Sales.CustomerID	Sales.ProductID	Sales.SaleDate	Sales.Quantity	Sales.TotalSaleValue
3	1	1	12 2023-02-28	1	1200.50

Products.ProductID	Products.ProductName	Products.Category	Products.Price
1	Laptop	Electronics	1200.50
2	Smartphone	Electronics	799.99
3	Headphones	Accessories	150.75

3.1. Total Sales for Electronics in 2023

sql

```sql
SELECT SUM(Sales.TotalSaleValue) AS TotalSales
FROM Sales
JOIN Products ON Sales.ProductID = Products.ProductID
WHERE Products.Category = 'Electronics' AND Sales.SaleDate
BETWEEN '2023-01-01' AND '2023-12-31';
```

This query joins the **Sales** and **Products** tables, filters for **Electronics** category products, and sums the **TotalSaleValue** for all transactions that occurred in **2023**.

3.2. Sales Transactions Between March 1st and March 15th, 2023, for Products Priced Above $100

sql

SELECT Sales.SaleID, Sales.SaleDate, Sales.TotalSaleValue, Products.ProductName
FROM Sales
JOIN Products ON Sales.ProductID = Products.ProductID
WHERE Sales.SaleDate BETWEEN '2023-03-01' AND '2023-03-15'
AND Products.Price > 100;

This query retrieves **Sales** transactions from **March 1st to March 15th, 2023**, and only includes **products priced above $100**. It returns details about the sales transaction ID, sale date, total value, and the product name.

In this chapter, we covered various techniques to filter data in SQL using the **WHERE** clause and its associated operators. We explored:

- Basic filtering operators like **AND, OR, LIKE, IN**, and **BETWEEN**.
- More advanced filtering using comparison operators (=, <, >, **BETWEEN, IN**) and logical operators (**AND, OR, NOT**).

- Real-world examples of filtering sales transactions based on date ranges and product categories.

In the next chapter, we will explore **sorting** and **ordering** query results to better analyze large datasets and present insights effectively.

CHAPTER 5: SORTING AND LIMITING RESULTS

Introduction to Sorting and Limiting Data

When working with large datasets, it's often necessary to sort the data in a specific order or limit the number of rows returned to make the analysis more manageable. SQL provides powerful tools to help you accomplish both of these tasks effectively.

In this chapter, we will cover:

- How to sort data using the **ORDER BY** clause.
- How to limit the number of rows returned using **LIMIT** and **OFFSET**.
- Real-world examples of sorting and limiting data to answer specific business questions.

1. Sorting Data Using the ORDER BY Clause

The **ORDER BY** clause allows you to sort query results based on one or more columns. Sorting can be done in either **ascending** (default) or **descending** order.

Basic Syntax:

sql

```
SELECT column1, column2, ...
FROM table_name
ORDER BY column_name [ASC|DESC];
```

- **ASC** (ascending) is the default. It sorts from the smallest to the largest value (alphabetically for text, numerically for numbers).
- **DESC** (descending) sorts from the largest to the smallest value (reverse alphabetical or numerical order).

1.1 Sorting in Ascending and Descending Order

To sort products by price in ascending order:

sql

```
SELECT ProductName, Price
FROM Products
ORDER BY Price ASC;
```

This query retrieves a list of products sorted by their price from lowest to highest.

To sort products by price in descending order:

sql

SELECT ProductName, Price

FROM Products

ORDER BY Price DESC;

This query sorts products by price from highest to lowest.

1.2 Sorting by Multiple Columns

You can also sort by multiple columns, specifying the order for each one. For example, if you want to sort products first by **Category** in ascending order, and then by **Price** in descending order (for products within the same category):

sql

SELECT ProductName, Category, Price

FROM Products

ORDER BY Category ASC, Price DESC;

This query first sorts products by **Category** alphabetically, and then within each category, it sorts by **Price** from highest to lowest.

2. Using LIMIT and OFFSET to Control the Number of Rows Returned

When querying large datasets, you may not need or want to retrieve all the rows at once. The **LIMIT** clause allows you to limit the number of rows returned, and the **OFFSET** clause allows you to skip a specific number of rows.

Basic Syntax:

sql

```
SELECT column1, column2, ...
FROM table_name
ORDER BY column_name
LIMIT number_of_rows OFFSET skip_number_of_rows;
```

- **LIMIT** restricts the number of rows returned.
- **OFFSET** skips a specified number of rows before starting to return results.

2.1 Using LIMIT to Restrict Rows

Example: Retrieve the top 5 most expensive products:

sql

```
SELECT ProductName, Price
FROM Products
ORDER BY Price DESC
LIMIT 5;
```

This query returns only the top 5 products, sorted by price in descending order.

2.2 Using LIMIT and OFFSET Together

The **OFFSET** clause is often used in combination with **LIMIT** to implement pagination. For example, if you want to retrieve products 6 through 10 from a list of products sorted by price:

sql

SELECT ProductName, Price

FROM Products

ORDER BY Price DESC

LIMIT 5 OFFSET 5;

This query skips the first 5 products and retrieves the next 5 products (i.e., products 6 to 10) sorted by price in descending order.

3. Real-World Example: Sorting Products by Price or Sales Volume

Let's apply the concepts from this chapter to a real-world scenario. Suppose we have an **e-commerce** database with the following two tables:

1. **Products Table**: Contains product details (ProductID, ProductName, Price, Category).
2. **Sales Table**: Contains sales data (SaleID, ProductID, QuantitySold, SaleDate).

We want to sort and limit the data to analyze different aspects of sales and product performance.

3.1. Sorting Products by Price

Let's say we want to identify the **top 10 most expensive products** in our catalog. Using the **ORDER BY** clause and **LIMIT**:

sql

```
SELECT ProductName, Price
FROM Products
ORDER BY Price DESC
LIMIT 10;
```

This query retrieves the **top 10 most expensive products** from the **Products** table, sorted from highest to lowest price.

3.2. Sorting Products by Sales Volume

Now, suppose we want to analyze the **top 5 products by sales volume**. We need to join the **Products** table with the **Sales** table to calculate the total sales quantity for each product. We'll then sort the results by **QuantitySold** in descending order to identify the most sold products.

sql

```
SELECT Products.ProductName, SUM(Sales.QuantitySold) AS
TotalSold
FROM Sales
JOIN Products ON Sales.ProductID = Products.ProductID
GROUP BY Products.ProductID
ORDER BY TotalSold DESC
LIMIT 5;
```

This query:

- Joins the **Sales** and **Products** tables.
- Uses the **SUM** function to calculate the total quantity sold for each product.
- Sorts the results by the total quantity sold in descending order.
- Limits the result to the **top 5 products by sales volume**.

3.3. Sales Data for Specific Time Period

Next, let's say we want to analyze the **top 10 products sold** during the month of **March 2023**. We will use a WHERE clause to filter the sales by date, and then apply sorting and limiting.

sql

```
SELECT Products.ProductName, SUM(Sales.QuantitySold) AS TotalSold
FROM Sales
JOIN Products ON Sales.ProductID = Products.ProductID
WHERE Sales.SaleDate BETWEEN '2023-03-01' AND '2023-03-31'
GROUP BY Products.ProductID
ORDER BY TotalSold DESC
LIMIT 10;
```

This query:

- Filters the sales data to include only those transactions that occurred in **March 2023**.
- Joins the **Sales** and **Products** tables.
- Calculates the total quantity sold for each product during this period.
- Sorts the results by total sales volume, and limits the output to the **top 10 products**.

In this chapter, we've covered how to:

- **Sort** data using the **ORDER BY** clause to organize results in ascending or descending order, and how to sort by multiple columns.
- Use the **LIMIT** and **OFFSET** clauses to control the number of rows returned and implement pagination.
- Apply these concepts to real-world scenarios, such as sorting products by price or sales volume, and limiting the results to focus on the most relevant data.

In the next chapter, we will explore how to **aggregate data** with SQL functions like **SUM, AVG, COUNT,** and **GROUP BY,** to answer more complex business questions using summary statistics.

CHAPTER 6: AGGREGATING DATA WITH SQL FUNCTIONS

Introduction to Aggregation and Grouping Data

When analyzing data, it's often useful to summarize information to extract key insights. SQL provides several aggregation functions that allow you to calculate summary statistics for your data, such as counting items, summing values, finding averages, and identifying minimum or maximum values. Additionally, the **GROUP BY** clause allows you to group your data into categories so that these aggregation functions can be applied to each group.

In this chapter, we will cover:

- How to use common **aggregation functions**: **COUNT, SUM, AVG, MIN**, and **MAX**.
- How to **group** data using the **GROUP BY** clause.
- Real-world examples of aggregating and grouping sales data by region or product type to derive meaningful business insights.

1. Using Aggregation Functions

SQL provides several built-in aggregation functions that allow you to perform common operations on data, such as:

- **COUNT()**: Counts the number of rows in a result set (or the number of non-NULL values in a column).
- **SUM()**: Calculates the total sum of a numeric column.
- **AVG()**: Computes the average of a numeric column.
- **MIN()**: Finds the minimum value in a column.
- **MAX()**: Finds the maximum value in a column.

1.1. Using COUNT()

The **COUNT()** function is used to count the number of rows or non-NULL values in a specific column.

Example: To count how many products are in the **Products** table:

sql

```
SELECT COUNT(*) AS TotalProducts
FROM Products;
```

This query returns the total number of rows (products) in the **Products** table.

To count the number of products in each category:

sql

```
SELECT Category, COUNT(*) AS ProductCount
FROM Products
GROUP BY Category;
```

This query returns the number of products in each category, grouped by the **Category** column.

1.2. Using SUM()

The **SUM()** function calculates the sum of a numeric column.

Example: To calculate the total sales amount from the **Sales** table:

sql

```
SELECT SUM(TotalSaleValue) AS TotalSales
FROM Sales;
```

This query returns the total value of all sales.

To calculate the total sales per region (assuming the **Sales** table has a **Region** column):

sql

```
SELECT Region, SUM(TotalSaleValue) AS TotalSales
FROM Sales
GROUP BY Region;
```

This query calculates the total sales for each **Region**.

1.3. Using AVG()

The **AVG()** function calculates the average of a numeric column.

Example: To calculate the average price of all products in the **Products** table:

sql

SELECT AVG(Price) AS AveragePrice

FROM Products;

This query returns the average price of all products.

To calculate the average sales value per transaction in the **Sales** table:

sql

SELECT AVG(TotalSaleValue) AS AverageTransaction

FROM Sales;

This query returns the average total sale value for all sales transactions.

1.4. Using MIN() and MAX()

The **MIN()** function finds the smallest value in a column, and the **MAX()** function finds the largest value.

Example: To find the minimum and maximum prices in the **Products** table:

sql

SELECT MIN(Price) AS MinimumPrice, MAX(Price) AS MaximumPrice

FROM Products;

This query returns the **lowest** and **highest** prices in the **Products** table.

To find the minimum and maximum sales value in the **Sales** table:

sql

SELECT   MIN(TotalSaleValue)   AS   MinimumSale, MAX(TotalSaleValue) AS MaximumSale
FROM Sales;

This query returns the **lowest** and **highest** total sales amounts in the **Sales** table.

2. Grouping Data with GROUP BY

The **GROUP BY** clause is used to group rows that have the same values in one or more columns. Aggregation functions like **COUNT()**, **SUM()**, **AVG()**, **MIN()**, and **MAX()** can then be applied to each group.

Basic Syntax:

sql

SELECT column1, column2, aggregate_function(column3)
FROM table_name
GROUP BY column1, column2;

2.1. Grouping by Single Column

Example: To calculate the total sales for each product category in the **Sales** table (assuming there's a **ProductCategory** column):

sql

SELECT ProductCategory, SUM(TotalSaleValue) AS TotalSales
FROM Sales
GROUP BY ProductCategory;

This query groups the sales data by **ProductCategory** and then calculates the **total sales** for each category.

2.2. Grouping by Multiple Columns

You can also group data by multiple columns. For example, if we wanted to calculate the total sales by both **Region** and **ProductCategory**, we would write:

sql

SELECT Region, ProductCategory, SUM(TotalSaleValue) AS TotalSales
FROM Sales
GROUP BY Region, ProductCategory;

This query groups the sales data by both **Region** and **ProductCategory**, and calculates the total sales for each combination of these two columns.

2.3. Using HAVING with GROUP BY

The **HAVING** clause is used to filter the results of a **GROUP BY** operation. It's similar to the **WHERE** clause, but **HAVING** filters groups, whereas **WHERE** filters individual rows before grouping.

Example: If we only wanted to include categories that had total sales greater than $10,000:

sql

```
SELECT ProductCategory, SUM(TotalSaleValue) AS TotalSales
FROM Sales
GROUP BY ProductCategory
HAVING SUM(TotalSaleValue) > 10000;
```

This query filters the grouped results and returns only those categories where the total sales exceed **$10,000**.

3. Real-World Example: Summarizing Sales Data by Region or Product Type

Let's now put everything together with a real-world example using the **Sales** and **Products** tables.

3.1. Summarizing Total Sales by Region

Let's say we want to summarize the total sales for each region, using the **Sales** table:

sql

```
SELECT Region, SUM(TotalSaleValue) AS TotalSales
```

FROM Sales

GROUP BY Region;

This query will return the total sales for each region, helping the business identify which regions generate the highest revenue.

3.2. Analyzing Average Sales by Product Type

Let's assume the **Products** table has a **Category** column, and we want to know the **average sales value** for each product category. We can use **AVG()** to calculate the average sales:

sql

SELECT Category, AVG(TotalSaleValue) AS AverageSale

FROM Sales

JOIN Products ON Sales.ProductID = Products.ProductID

GROUP BY Category;

This query joins the **Sales** and **Products** tables, groups the data by **Category**, and calculates the **average sale value** for each product category.

3.3. Counting Sales Transactions by Product Type

If we wanted to know how many transactions were made for each product category, we could use **COUNT()** to count the number of sales transactions for each category:

sql

```
SELECT Category, COUNT(*) AS TransactionCount
FROM Sales
JOIN Products ON Sales.ProductID = Products.ProductID
GROUP BY Category;
```

This query counts the number of transactions for each **product category**, providing insights into the volume of sales per category.

4. Summary

In this chapter, we learned how to aggregate and group data in SQL to summarize large datasets. Specifically, we covered:

- **Aggregation functions**: **COUNT()**, **SUM()**, **AVG()**, **MIN()**, and **MAX()**.
- **GROUP BY**: How to group data by one or more columns and apply aggregation functions to these groups.
- **HAVING**: How to filter results after grouping with **HAVING**.
- Real-world examples of summarizing sales data by region or product category, and using **COUNT()** and **AVG()** to analyze sales performance.

In the next chapter, we will dive into **joins**—how to combine data from multiple tables to answer more complex business questions and perform deeper analysis.

CHAPTER 7: ADVANCED FILTERING WITH HAVING

Introduction to Filtering Grouped Data

In SQL, filtering data is a key part of analysis. While the **WHERE** clause filters rows before they are grouped, the **HAVING** clause filters the results after they have been grouped. This distinction is critical when performing aggregations, as **HAVING** allows you to apply conditions on the result of an aggregation, whereas **WHERE** only applies to individual rows.

In this chapter, we will cover:

- How to use the **HAVING** clause to filter grouped data.
- The differences between **WHERE** and **HAVING**.
- Real-world examples of filtering aggregated sales data to focus on specific insights.

1. Understanding the HAVING Clause

The **HAVING** clause is used in SQL to filter results after they have been grouped by the **GROUP BY** clause. This makes it particularly useful when you need to filter based on an aggregation or summary statistic (e.g., total sales, average price, etc.). The **HAVING** clause can only be used in combination with **GROUP BY** and aggregation functions.

Basic Syntax:

sql

SELECT column1, column2, aggregate_function(column3)

FROM table_name

GROUP BY column1, column2

HAVING aggregate_function(column3) condition;

- **HAVING** applies a filter to the result of an aggregation.
- **aggregate_function(column3)** is the aggregation you're applying, such as **SUM()**, **AVG()**, or **COUNT()**.
- **condition** is the condition that filters the grouped data.

1.1. Using HAVING to Filter Aggregated Data

For example, if we want to find the **regions** where the total sales exceed $10,000, we would use **HAVING** in combination with **SUM()**:

sql

SELECT Region, SUM(SalesAmount) AS TotalSales

FROM Sales

GROUP BY Region

HAVING SUM(SalesAmount) > 10000;

This query:

- Groups the sales data by **Region**.
- Calculates the **total sales** for each region.
- Filters the results to include only regions where total sales exceed $10,000.

2. Differences Between WHERE and HAVING

Both **WHERE** and **HAVING** are used to filter data, but they are applied at different stages of the query process:

- **WHERE**: Filters **rows** before grouping and aggregation occur. It applies to individual records, meaning it operates on the raw data before any **GROUP BY** or aggregation functions are applied.

  Example: Filtering rows where sales are greater than $50 before grouping:

  sql

  ```
  SELECT Region, SUM(SalesAmount) AS TotalSales
  FROM Sales
  WHERE SalesAmount > 50
  GROUP BY Region;
  ```

  In this case, the query filters individual sales transactions where **SalesAmount** is greater than 50 before grouping them by **Region** and summing them.

- **HAVING**: Filters the results **after** grouping and aggregation have been applied. It works with aggregated values or summary statistics.

Example: Filtering regions where total sales (after grouping) exceed $10,000:

sql

```
SELECT Region, SUM(SalesAmount) AS TotalSales
FROM Sales
GROUP BY Region
HAVING SUM(SalesAmount) > 10000;
```

In this case, the query first groups the data by **Region**, calculates the total sales per region, and then applies the **HAVING** filter to include only those regions where total sales exceed $10,000.

2.1. Key Differences

- **WHERE**: Filters rows before aggregation. Can be used on individual columns in a table.
- **HAVING**: Filters results after aggregation. Can be used on the results of aggregation functions.

3. Real-World Example: Analyzing Average Sales Per Product Type

Let's explore a real-world scenario where we analyze sales data by product type. We'll calculate the **average sales** per **product type** and filter out those product types with an average sales value below a certain threshold using **HAVING**.

Assume we have two tables:

1. **Products Table**: Contains product details (ProductID, ProductName, Category).
2. **Sales Table**: Contains sales data (SaleID, ProductID, SalesAmount, SaleDate).

3.1. Calculating Average Sales Per Product Category

We want to calculate the **average sales amount** for each **product category** and display only those categories where the average sales are greater than $200.

sql

```
SELECT    Products.Category,    AVG(Sales.SalesAmount)    AS
AverageSales
FROM Sales
JOIN Products ON Sales.ProductID = Products.ProductID
GROUP BY Products.Category
HAVING AVG(Sales.SalesAmount) > 200;
```

This query:

- Joins the **Sales** and **Products** tables based on **ProductID**.
- Groups the data by **Category** (from the **Products** table).
- Calculates the **average sales amount** for each product category using the **AVG()** function.
- Filters the results with **HAVING** to include only product categories where the **average sales** exceed **$200**.

3.2. Analyzing Sales Data for High-Performing Product Categories

Let's assume we want to identify which product categories have a **total sales** above $10,000 and where the **average sales** per transaction exceed $200. This would require using both **SUM()** and **AVG()** with **HAVING**.

sql

```
SELECT Products.Category,
    SUM(Sales.SalesAmount) AS TotalSales,
    AVG(Sales.SalesAmount) AS AverageSales
FROM Sales
JOIN Products ON Sales.ProductID = Products.ProductID
GROUP BY Products.Category
HAVING SUM(Sales.SalesAmount) > 10000
    AND AVG(Sales.SalesAmount) > 200;
```

This query:

- Groups the data by **Category**.
- Calculates both the **total sales** and **average sales** for each category.
- Filters the results to include only categories where:
  - **Total sales** exceed **$10,000**.
  - **Average sales per transaction** exceed **$200**.

3.3. More Complex Filtering with Multiple Aggregations

You can also combine multiple conditions in the **HAVING** clause to filter on different aggregations simultaneously. For instance, if we wanted to find categories with total sales over $5,000 and average sales per transaction greater than $150, we could write:

sql

```
SELECT Products.Category,
    SUM(Sales.SalesAmount) AS TotalSales,
    AVG(Sales.SalesAmount) AS AverageSales
FROM Sales
JOIN Products ON Sales.ProductID = Products.ProductID
GROUP BY Products.Category
HAVING SUM(Sales.SalesAmount) > 5000
    AND AVG(Sales.SalesAmount) > 150;
```

This query returns product categories that meet both conditions:

- **Total sales** exceed **$5,000**.
- **Average sales** per transaction exceed **$150**.

In this chapter, we learned how to use the **HAVING** clause to filter data after aggregation. Key points include:

- The **HAVING** clause is used to filter aggregated data after **GROUP BY**.
- **WHERE** filters rows before aggregation, whereas **HAVING** filters the results of aggregation.
- Real-world examples showed how to use **HAVING** to filter aggregated sales data, such as finding product categories with total sales above a threshold or average sales greater than a specific value.

Next, in **Chapter 8**, we will dive into **joins** and how to combine data from multiple tables to derive more meaningful insights, a critical skill for data analysts working with relational databases.

CHAPTER 8: COMBINING DATA FROM MULTIPLE TABLES WITH JOINS

Introduction to SQL Joins

In the world of relational databases, data is often spread across multiple tables. To perform comprehensive analysis, you need to combine data from these tables. This is where SQL **joins** come into play. A **join** allows you to retrieve data from two or more tables based on a related column, typically a primary key in one table and a foreign key in another.

In this chapter, we will cover:

- The **different types of SQL joins**: **INNER JOIN**, **LEFT JOIN**, **RIGHT JOIN**, and **FULL JOIN**.
- How to **combine multiple tables** to analyze relationships between different entities (e.g., customers, products, orders).
- A **real-world example** of combining **sales data** and **customer data** to analyze purchasing patterns.

1. Types of SQL Joins

There are four primary types of joins in SQL: **INNER JOIN**, **LEFT JOIN**, **RIGHT JOIN**, and **FULL JOIN**. Each type determines how rows from the joined tables are selected.

1.1. INNER JOIN

The **INNER JOIN** returns only the rows where there is a match between the columns in both tables. If there is no match, the row is excluded from the result.

Syntax:

sql

SELECT column1, column2, ...
FROM table1
INNER JOIN table2 ON table1.common_column = table2.common_column;

Example: Let's assume we have two tables:

- **Orders** (OrderID, CustomerID, ProductID, OrderDate, Quantity)
- **Customers** (CustomerID, Name, Address, Email)

To retrieve a list of all orders along with customer details, you would use an **INNER JOIN** on the **CustomerID**:

sql

SELECT Orders.OrderID, Customers.Name, Orders.ProductID, Orders.Quantity

FROM Orders

INNER JOIN Customers ON Orders.CustomerID = Customers.CustomerID;

This query will return only the rows where there is a match between the **CustomerID** in both the **Orders** and **Customers** tables.

1.2. LEFT JOIN (or LEFT OUTER JOIN)

The **LEFT JOIN** returns all rows from the left table (the first table) and the matching rows from the right table (the second table). If there is no match, **NULL** values are returned for columns from the right table.

Syntax:

sql

SELECT column1, column2, ...

FROM table1

LEFT JOIN table2 ON table1.common_column = table2.common_column;

Example: Using the same **Orders** and **Customers** tables, let's find all customers, including those who have not made any orders:

sql

SELECT Customers.Name, Orders.OrderID

FROM Customers

LEFT JOIN Orders ON Customers.CustomerID =
Orders.CustomerID;

This query will return all customers and their associated **OrderID** (if any). Customers who haven't placed any orders will still appear in the result, but with **NULL** in the **OrderID** column.

1.3. RIGHT JOIN (or RIGHT OUTER JOIN)

The **RIGHT JOIN** is similar to the **LEFT JOIN**, but it returns all rows from the right table (the second table) and the matching rows from the left table (the first table). If there is no match, **NULL** values are returned for columns from the left table.

Syntax:

sql

SELECT column1, column2, ...

FROM table1

RIGHT JOIN table2 ON table1.common_column =
table2.common_column;

Example: Let's assume the **Orders** table has a **ProductID** that is not necessarily listed in the **Products** table. To retrieve all orders, along with product details, even for products that are not found in the **Products** table, you can use a **RIGHT JOIN**:

sql

SELECT Orders.OrderID, Products.ProductName

FROM Orders

RIGHT   JOIN   Products   ON   Orders.ProductID   =
Products.ProductID;

This query will return all products and their associated **OrderID** (if any). Products with no orders will have **NULL** in the **OrderID** column.

1.4. FULL JOIN (or FULL OUTER JOIN)

The **FULL JOIN** returns all rows when there is a match in one of the tables. If there is no match, the missing side will have **NULL** values. This join is useful when you want to ensure that all rows from both tables are included in the result.

Syntax:

sql

SELECT column1, column2, ...

FROM table1

FULL   JOIN   table2   ON   table1.common_column   =
table2.common_column;

Example: If you want to retrieve all customers and all orders, whether or not there is a match between the two, use a **FULL JOIN**:

sql

SELECT Customers.Name, Orders.OrderID
FROM Customers
FULL JOIN Orders ON Customers.CustomerID =
Orders.CustomerID;
This query will return:

- All customers, even if they haven't placed an order.
- All orders, even if they haven't been associated with a customer.

2. Combining Multiple Tables for Data Analysis

SQL joins allow you to explore relationships between multiple tables. Let's look at a real-world example where we combine **sales data** and **customer data** to analyze purchasing patterns.

2.1. Example: Combining Sales and Customer Data

Let's assume we have the following two tables:

1. **Customers** (CustomerID, Name, Email, Location)
2. **Sales** (SaleID, CustomerID, ProductID, SalesAmount, Date)

We want to analyze purchasing patterns by linking the **Sales** table with the **Customers** table based on **CustomerID**.

Goal: We want to find the total sales per customer and display it alongside the customer's name and location.

Query:

sql

SELECT   Customers.Name,   Customers.Location,
SUM(Sales.SalesAmount) AS TotalSales
FROM Sales
INNER   JOIN   Customers   ON   Sales.CustomerID   =
Customers.CustomerID
GROUP BY Customers.Name, Customers.Location;
This query:

- Joins the **Sales** and **Customers** tables using **INNER JOIN**.
- Groups the result by **Customer Name** and **Location**.
- Calculates the **SUM** of **SalesAmount** for each customer.

The result will show each customer's total sales along with their name and location.

2.2. Example: Identifying Customers Who Made Multiple Purchases

Let's modify the query to find customers who made multiple purchases and whose total sales amount is over $500. We'll use **HAVING** to filter customers with total sales above $500.

Query:

sql

```
SELECT    Customers.Name,    SUM(Sales.SalesAmount)    AS
TotalSales, COUNT(Sales.SaleID) AS PurchaseCount
FROM Sales
INNER    JOIN    Customers    ON    Sales.CustomerID    =
Customers.CustomerID
GROUP BY Customers.Name
HAVING        COUNT(Sales.SaleID)        >        1        AND
SUM(Sales.SalesAmount) > 500;
```

This query:

- Joins the **Sales** and **Customers** tables.
- Groups the data by **Customer Name**.
- Calculates the total sales and the number of purchases (using **COUNT(SaleID)**).
- Filters the results to show only customers who have made more than one purchase and whose total sales exceed $500.

3. Practical Tips for Using Joins

- **Use Aliases for Readability:** When working with multiple tables, use table aliases (short names) to make your queries more readable. For example:

  sql

  ```
  SELECT c.Name, o.OrderID
  ```

FROM Customers c

JOIN Orders o ON c.CustomerID = o.CustomerID;

- **Consider Performance:** Joins can be resource-intensive, especially with large datasets. To optimize performance:
  - Ensure the join column is indexed.
  - Use appropriate filtering in the **WHERE** clause to reduce the dataset before performing joins.
- **Handling NULLs:** Remember that outer joins (**LEFT JOIN, RIGHT JOIN, FULL JOIN**) will return **NULL** for unmatched rows. You can use **COALESCE()** or **IFNULL()** to replace **NULL** values with defaults if needed.

In this chapter, we:

- Covered the four types of SQL joins: **INNER JOIN, LEFT JOIN, RIGHT JOIN**, and **FULL JOIN**.
- Discussed how to use these joins to combine data from multiple tables.
- Explored real-world examples, such as combining **sales** and **customer** data to analyze purchasing patterns.
- Learned how to filter, group, and aggregate joined data to derive insights.

Next, in **Chapter 9**, we will look at **subqueries**—queries within queries—that can help solve more complex data problems and improve analytical workflows.

CHAPTER 9: SUBQUERIES: QUERIES WITHIN QUERIES

Introduction to Subqueries

A **subquery** (also known as an inner query or nested query) is a query placed inside another query. Subqueries are incredibly useful for breaking down complex data retrieval tasks into smaller, more manageable pieces. They allow you to perform operations that would be difficult or impossible with a single query, such as filtering data based on aggregated results, dynamically selecting values, or comparing results across multiple datasets.

A subquery can be placed in several parts of a main query, typically in the **SELECT**, **FROM**, or **WHERE** clause. When used effectively, subqueries can simplify SQL code and make it more readable, though they can also impact performance in certain cases (especially with large datasets).

In this chapter, we will cover:

- **What subqueries are** and how they work.
- **How to use subqueries** in the **SELECT**, **FROM**, and **WHERE** clauses.
- A **real-world example** of using subqueries to identify **top-selling products**.

1. Subqueries in SQL

A subquery is any query nested inside another SQL query. It can return a single value (scalar subquery), a list of values (in a column), or a table of results (in the case of **multi-row subqueries**). Subqueries allow you to use results from one query as inputs to another.

1.1. Types of Subqueries

Subqueries can be categorized by where they appear in the main query:

- **Scalar subqueries**: Return a single value.
- **Column subqueries**: Return a set of values from a single column.
- **Row subqueries**: Return multiple columns in a single row.
- **Table subqueries**: Return multiple rows and columns (acting like a derived table).

Let's now look at subqueries in their various forms.

2. Using Subqueries in the SELECT Clause

A **subquery in the SELECT clause** is used when you need to compute a value that is derived from another query. This can be useful for calculations or aggregations based on related data.

Example:

Imagine you want to find the **sales of each product**, along with the **average sales for all products**. You can use a subquery in the **SELECT** clause to calculate the overall average sales.

Tables:

- **Products** (ProductID, ProductName)
- **Sales** (SaleID, ProductID, SaleAmount)

Query:

sql

```
SELECT
    ProductName,
    SUM(SaleAmount) AS TotalSales,
    (SELECT AVG(SaleAmount) FROM Sales) AS AvgSales
FROM Products
JOIN Sales ON Products.ProductID = Sales.ProductID
GROUP BY ProductName;
```

In this query:

- The subquery (SELECT AVG(SaleAmount) FROM Sales) calculates the average sales across all products, and this value is included in the result for each product.

3. Using Subqueries in the FROM Clause

A **subquery in the FROM clause** is often referred to as a **derived table**. The result of the subquery is treated as a temporary table, and the main query can select from this "virtual table." This is useful when you need to perform multiple operations on the same set of data before retrieving the final result.

Example:

Let's say you want to calculate the **total sales per product** and find the **average sales per product**. Instead of calculating total sales and averages separately, you can use a subquery in the **FROM** clause to simplify the query.

Query:

sql

```
SELECT
    ProductName,
    TotalSales,
    AVG(TotalSales) AS AvgProductSales
FROM
    (SELECT ProductName, SUM(SaleAmount) AS TotalSales
     FROM Products
     JOIN Sales ON Products.ProductID = Sales.ProductID
     GROUP BY ProductName) AS SalesSummary
GROUP BY ProductName, TotalSales;
```

Here, the subquery:

- Aggregates sales data by product, creating a temporary table called SalesSummary.
- The outer query then calculates the **average** of these **total sales** values.

4. Using Subqueries in the WHERE Clause

The **WHERE clause** is the most common place to use subqueries. Subqueries in the **WHERE** clause allow you to filter results based on the outcome of another query. This is particularly useful when you need to:

- Compare values across different tables.
- Filter data based on aggregate values.

4.1. Scalar Subquery in WHERE Clause

A **scalar subquery** returns a single value, and you can use it in the **WHERE** clause for comparison purposes.

Example:

Let's assume you want to find all products that have sales greater than the **average sales** for all products.

Query:

sql

```
SELECT ProductName, SUM(SaleAmount) AS TotalSales
FROM Products
JOIN Sales ON Products.ProductID = Sales.ProductID
GROUP BY ProductName
HAVING  SUM(SaleAmount)  >  (SELECT  AVG(SaleAmount)
FROM Sales);
```

In this query:

- The subquery (SELECT AVG(SaleAmount) FROM Sales) returns the average sales across all products.
- The outer query then filters products whose **total sales** are greater than this average.

4.2. Using IN with Subqueries

You can also use the **IN** operator with subqueries when you need to filter based on a list of values returned by a subquery.

Example:

To find all **customers** who have made **purchases** for products from a specific category, you could use a subquery in the **WHERE** clause.

sql

```
SELECT CustomerID, Name
FROM Customers
```

WHERE CustomerID IN

 (SELECT CustomerID FROM Sales WHERE ProductID IN

  (SELECT ProductID FROM Products WHERE Category =
'Electronics'));

In this query:

- The innermost subquery finds all **ProductID** values for products in the **Electronics** category.
- The middle subquery filters all sales for those products.
- The outer query finds customers who have made purchases for those products.

5. Real-World Example: Identifying Top-Selling Products Using Subqueries

Let's look at a **real-world example** using subqueries to identify the **top-selling products** in a retail environment. In this case, we want to find the products whose total sales are above the average sales for all products.

Tables:

- **Products** (ProductID, ProductName, Category)
- **Sales** (SaleID, ProductID, SaleAmount)

We will:

1. Aggregate the **Sales** data by product to calculate **total sales**.

2. Use a subquery to calculate the **average sales** across all products.

3. Compare each product's **total sales** with the **average sales**.

Query:

sql

SELECT ProductName, SUM(SaleAmount) AS TotalSales
FROM Products
JOIN Sales ON Products.ProductID = Sales.ProductID
GROUP BY ProductName
HAVING SUM(SaleAmount) >
   (SELECT AVG(SaleAmount) FROM Sales);
Here:

- The subquery (SELECT AVG(SaleAmount) FROM Sales) calculates the **average sales** across all products.
- The outer query finds the **ProductName** and their **total sales**, filtering out products with sales below the average.

6. Best Practices for Using Subqueries

- **Optimize Performance:** Subqueries can sometimes lead to performance bottlenecks, especially with large datasets. Consider:

- o Using **joins** where possible, as they tend to be more efficient.
- o Avoid using subqueries in the **SELECT** clause if you don't need to retrieve aggregated data.
- **Use Aliases for Subqueries:** When using subqueries in the **FROM** clause, always alias the subquery as a table for clarity.

Example:

sql

```
SELECT ProductName, TotalSales
FROM
    (SELECT ProductID, SUM(SaleAmount) AS TotalSales
     FROM Sales
     GROUP BY ProductID) AS SalesSummary
JOIN    Products    ON    SalesSummary.ProductID    =
Products.ProductID;
```

- **Keep it Simple:** While subqueries are powerful, they can also make queries harder to read and debug. Use them when necessary, but aim for clarity.

In this chapter, we:

- Explored the concept of **subqueries** and their use in SQL.

- Covered the three common places to use subqueries: **SELECT**, **FROM**, and **WHERE** clauses.
- Looked at real-world examples, including how to identify **top-selling products** using a subquery.
- Discussed best practices for optimizing and simplifying subqueries.

In **Chapter 10**, we will dive into **window functions**—advanced SQL techniques that allow you to perform calculations across sets of rows while retaining the individual row context.

CHAPTER 10: USING CASE STATEMENTS FOR CONDITIONAL LOGIC

Introduction to the CASE Statement in SQL

The **CASE** statement is a powerful conditional expression in SQL that allows you to add logic to your queries. It works like an "if-else" structure in programming languages, enabling you to perform conditional checks within SQL queries and return different values based on those conditions.

In SQL, the **CASE** statement is often used to:

- **Create dynamic categories** based on data values (e.g., high, medium, low sales).
- **Conditionally modify the output** of a query without altering the underlying data.
- **Perform calculations** that depend on certain conditions (e.g., applying different tax rates based on location).

The **CASE** expression can be used in various parts of SQL queries, such as:

- **SELECT**: To modify the result set based on conditions.
- **WHERE**: To add conditional filters.
- **ORDER BY**: To sort results dynamically.

This chapter will explain:

- How to use the **CASE** statement for adding conditional logic to your queries.
- A **real-world example** of categorizing products based on **sales performance** (e.g., high, medium, and low sales).

1. Syntax of the CASE Statement

There are two main forms of the **CASE** statement in SQL:

1. **Simple CASE Expression**: It compares an expression to a series of values.

    Syntax:

    sql

    ```
    CASE expression
        WHEN value1 THEN result1
        WHEN value2 THEN result2
        ELSE result_default
    END
    ```

    - ○ **expression**: The value you want to check.
    - ○ **WHEN**: Specifies a value to compare with the expression.

- o **THEN**: Defines the result to return if the condition is true.

  - o **ELSE**: (Optional) Specifies a default result if none of the conditions match.

2. **Searched CASE Expression**: It allows more complex conditions using logical expressions.

Syntax:

sql

```
CASE
    WHEN condition1 THEN result1
    WHEN condition2 THEN result2
    ELSE result_default
END
```

- o **WHEN**: Defines a condition to test.
- o **THEN**: Defines the result if the condition is true.
- o **ELSE**: (Optional) A default result if no conditions are true.

2. Using the CASE Statement in the SELECT Clause

The **SELECT** clause is a common place to use the **CASE** statement, allowing you to dynamically modify the data returned in your result set based on certain conditions.

Example 1: Creating Categories Based on Sales Performance

Imagine you have a sales database with the following structure:

- **Products** (ProductID, ProductName, Category)
- **Sales** (SaleID, ProductID, SaleAmount)

You want to categorize products based on their **total sales**:

- High sales: Total sales > $100,000
- Medium sales: Total sales between $50,000 and $100,000
- Low sales: Total sales < $50,000

You can use the **CASE** statement to create these categories dynamically in the result set.

Query:

sql

```
SELECT
   ProductName,
   SUM(SaleAmount) AS TotalSales,
   CASE
      WHEN SUM(SaleAmount) > 100000 THEN 'High Sales'
      WHEN SUM(SaleAmount) BETWEEN 50000 AND 100000
THEN 'Medium Sales'
      ELSE 'Low Sales'
   END AS SalesCategory
```

FROM Products

JOIN Sales ON Products.ProductID = Sales.ProductID

GROUP BY ProductName;

Explanation:

- The **SUM(SaleAmount)** calculates the total sales for each product.
- The **CASE** statement evaluates the total sales for each product and assigns a category based on the sales amount.
- Products with sales above $100,000 are categorized as **High Sales**, those with sales between $50,000 and $100,000 as **Medium Sales**, and the rest as **Low Sales**.

3. Using the CASE Statement in the WHERE Clause

The **WHERE** clause can also use the **CASE** statement to apply conditional filters. This is useful when you want to filter rows based on calculated conditions rather than static values.

Example 2: Filtering Based on Conditional Sales Performance

Suppose you want to get a list of products that fall into the **High Sales** category, but only for those products that have made at least **50 sales transactions**.

Query:

sql

```
SELECT
    ProductName,
    SUM(SaleAmount) AS TotalSales,
    COUNT(SaleID) AS TotalTransactions
FROM Products
JOIN Sales ON Products.ProductID = Sales.ProductID
GROUP BY ProductName
HAVING
    SUM(SaleAmount) > 100000
    AND COUNT(SaleID) >= 50;
```

Here, we use a standard **HAVING** clause to filter out products with low sales, but this could also be done conditionally by introducing a **CASE** statement within the HAVING clause if the conditions were more complex.

4. Using the CASE Statement in the ORDER BY Clause

The **ORDER BY** clause can also be enhanced with **CASE** statements to dynamically sort the data based on conditional logic. This is particularly useful when you want to rank items in a custom way, such as sorting by performance tiers (e.g., high, medium, low sales).

Example 3: Sorting Products by Sales Performance Category

Suppose you want to order products so that **High Sales** products appear first, followed by **Medium Sales**, and then **Low Sales**. You can use a **CASE** statement in the **ORDER BY** clause to achieve this.

Query:

sql

```
SELECT
    ProductName,
    SUM(SaleAmount) AS TotalSales
FROM Products
JOIN Sales ON Products.ProductID = Sales.ProductID
GROUP BY ProductName
ORDER BY
    CASE
        WHEN SUM(SaleAmount) > 100000 THEN 1
        WHEN SUM(SaleAmount) BETWEEN 50000 AND 100000 THEN 2
        ELSE 3
    END;
```

Explanation:

- The **CASE** statement assigns numerical values (1, 2, 3) to each sales category (High, Medium, Low).
- The query then orders the products based on these values, ensuring that products with high sales are displayed first,

followed by those with medium sales, and then those with low sales.

5. Real-World Example: Dynamic Sales Category

In a **retail business**, categorizing products based on their sales performance helps identify the most profitable items, track inventory levels, and make decisions about product promotions. Using the **CASE** statement in SQL allows businesses to dynamically categorize products and easily segment them based on sales volume, pricing, or other factors.

Let's revisit our earlier example with a more detailed context:

Scenario: You are a data analyst at a retail company that wants to categorize products into sales tiers: **High**, **Medium**, and **Low** based on their performance in the last quarter. You will:

- Retrieve the sales data for each product.
- Calculate the total sales for each product.
- Categorize them based on predefined sales thresholds.

SQL Query:

sql

```
SELECT
    ProductName,
    SUM(SaleAmount) AS TotalSales,
```

```
CASE
    WHEN SUM(SaleAmount) > 100000 THEN 'High Sales'
    WHEN SUM(SaleAmount) BETWEEN 50000 AND 100000
THEN 'Medium Sales'
    ELSE 'Low Sales'
  END AS SalesCategory
FROM Products
JOIN Sales ON Products.ProductID = Sales.ProductID
WHERE SaleDate BETWEEN '2023-01-01' AND '2023-03-31'
GROUP BY ProductName;
```

Result: This query categorizes products based on their **sales performance** for the first quarter of 2023. It uses the **CASE** statement to group products into **High Sales**, **Medium Sales**, and **Low Sales**, which can then be used for analysis, reporting, and decision-making.

6. Best Practices for Using the CASE Statement

- **Keep Conditions Simple**: While you can add complex logic in the **CASE** statement, try to keep the conditions simple for readability and performance.
- **Use Else Carefully**: The **ELSE** part of the **CASE** statement is optional but useful for ensuring all scenarios are covered. If omitted, the query will return NULL for rows that do not match any condition.

- **Avoid Overuse in WHERE/ORDER BY**: Using **CASE** in the **WHERE** or **ORDER BY** clauses can be helpful but may negatively affect performance if overused, especially in large datasets.

In this chapter, we covered:

- The **CASE** statement as a way to introduce conditional logic in SQL.
- The syntax for **simple** and **searched** CASE expressions.
- How to use **CASE** in the **SELECT, WHERE**, and **ORDER BY** clauses for flexible, dynamic queries.
- Real-world applications of using **CASE** for categorizing data, such as segmenting products by sales performance.

In **Chapter 11**, we will dive into **window functions**, which allow you to perform calculations across a set of rows related to the current row without changing the structure of the result set.

CHAPTER 11: WORKING WITH DATE AND TIME IN SQL

Introduction to Date and Time Functions in SQL

In data analysis, handling **date and time** data is crucial for analyzing trends, making time-based comparisons, and performing operations like filtering, grouping, and aggregating data. SQL provides a variety of **date and time functions** that allow you to work with these types of data efficiently.

This chapter will cover:

- Key **SQL date functions** such as DATE, TIMESTAMP, NOW, DATE_ADD, and DATE_SUB.
- How to **extract specific date/time components** (e.g., year, month, day).
- A **real-world example** of using date functions to analyze **monthly sales trends** and filter sales by year.

1. SQL Date Functions

SQL provides several functions for manipulating and querying date and time data:

1. **DATE**: Returns the date part of a **DATE** or **DATETIME** value (i.e., year, month, and day). This function discards the time component.

   o **Example**:

   sql

   SELECT DATE('2023-03-15 10:00:00');

   Result: 2023-03-15

2. **TIMESTAMP**: Returns the current date and time as a **TIMESTAMP** value, which includes both the date and the time.

   o **Example**:

   sql

   SELECT TIMESTAMP('2023-03-15 10:00:00');

   Result: 2023-03-15 10:00:00

3. **NOW()**: Returns the current **date and time** (the exact moment when the query is executed).

   o **Example**:

   sql

SELECT NOW();

Result: 2023-03-15 10:30:22 (varies with execution time)

4. **DATE_ADD()**: Adds a specified **time interval** to a **date**. You can add days, months, years, or other time units.
   o **Example**:

   sql

   SELECT DATE_ADD('2023-03-15', INTERVAL 10 DAY);

   Result: 2023-03-25

5. **DATE_SUB()**: Subtracts a specified **time interval** from a **date**. Similar to DATE_ADD(), but subtracts instead of adding.
   o **Example**:

   sql

   SELECT DATE_SUB('2023-03-15', INTERVAL 1 MONTH);

Result: 2023-02-15

2. Extracting Specific Date/Time Components

SQL also allows you to extract specific components of a **DATE** or **DATETIME** value. This is useful for breaking down dates into parts, such as the year, month, day, or even the day of the week.

Here are some common functions for extracting components:

1. **YEAR()**: Extracts the year part of a **DATE** or **DATETIME**.
   - ○ **Example**:

   sql

   ```
   SELECT YEAR('2023-03-15');
   ```

   Result: 2023

2. **MONTH()**: Extracts the month part of a **DATE** or **DATETIME**.
   - ○ **Example**:

   sql

   ```
   SELECT MONTH('2023-03-15');
   ```

Result: 3 (March)

3. **DAY()**: Extracts the day part of a **DATE** or **DATETIME**.
   o **Example**:

   sql

   SELECT DAY('2023-03-15');

   Result: 15

4. **WEEK()**: Extracts the week number of the year (1 to 53).
   o **Example**:

   sql

   SELECT WEEK('2023-03-15');

   Result: 11 (the 11th week of the year)

5. **DAYOFWEEK()**: Extracts the day of the week (1 to 7, where 1 = Sunday, 7 = Saturday).
   o **Example**:

   sql

   SELECT DAYOFWEEK('2023-03-15');

Result: 4 (Wednesday)

6. **HOUR(), MINUTE(), SECOND()**: Extracts the respective time components from a **DATETIME** or **TIMESTAMP**.

   o **Example**:

   sql

   SELECT HOUR('2023-03-15 10:30:00');

   Result: 10 (hour)

3. Real-World Example: Analyzing Monthly Sales Trends

Let's walk through a real-world scenario where date functions are used to analyze **sales trends** in a retail database. Assume you have the following tables:

- **Sales**: Contains sales transaction data (SaleID, ProductID, SaleAmount, SaleDate)
- **Products**: Contains product information (ProductID, ProductName)

We want to analyze **monthly sales trends** and filter the data by year to understand sales patterns over time. This involves using **DATE functions** to extract the year and month, and then aggregating the sales data for each month.

Step 1: Query to Extract Year and Month from SaleDate

We'll start by extracting the **year** and **month** from the SaleDate field and then group the sales by these components to calculate the total sales for each month.

Query:

sql

```
SELECT
    YEAR(SaleDate) AS SalesYear,
    MONTH(SaleDate) AS SalesMonth,
    SUM(SaleAmount) AS TotalSales
FROM Sales
WHERE YEAR(SaleDate) = 2023   -- Filtering for sales data in 2023
GROUP BY SalesYear, SalesMonth
ORDER BY SalesYear, SalesMonth;
```

Explanation:

- **YEAR(SaleDate)**: Extracts the year from the sale date.
- **MONTH(SaleDate)**: Extracts the month from the sale date.
- **SUM(SaleAmount)**: Calculates the total sales for each year and month.
- **GROUP BY SalesYear, SalesMonth**: Groups the data by year and month to aggregate the sales.
- **WHERE YEAR(SaleDate) = 2023**: Filters the data to include only sales from the year 2023.

Example Output:

SalesYear SalesMonth TotalSales

SalesYear	SalesMonth	TotalSales
2023	1	120000
2023	2	95000
2023	3	110000
...	...	...

Step 2: Analyzing Monthly Sales Trends

To analyze the sales trend, we can plot these monthly sales totals on a graph or visualize them in a dashboard. This would allow you to identify which months had peak sales and which months were slower. For example, if you notice a dip in sales in February, you may look into factors like seasonal variations or marketing efforts during that period.

4. Advanced Date Operations

In addition to the basic date functions, SQL also allows you to perform **advanced operations** using **DATE_ADD()**, **DATE_SUB()**, and custom intervals.

Example 1: Adding and Subtracting Dates

You can use DATE_ADD() and DATE_SUB() to compute dates relative to a given date. For instance, if you want to find sales data from **the previous 30 days**:

Query:

sql

```
SELECT
  ProductID,
  SUM(SaleAmount) AS TotalSales
FROM Sales
WHERE SaleDate >= DATE_SUB(NOW(), INTERVAL 30 DAY)
GROUP BY ProductID;
```

Explanation:

- NOW() retrieves the current date and time.
- DATE_SUB(NOW(), INTERVAL 30 DAY) calculates the date 30 days before the current date.
- This query retrieves sales data for the last 30 days, grouped by product.

Example 2: Finding Sales for the Current Quarter

To find sales for the current quarter, you can use date manipulation to get the first day of the quarter and the last day of the quarter:

Query:

sql

```
SELECT
  ProductID,
  SUM(SaleAmount) AS TotalSales
FROM Sales
WHERE SaleDate BETWEEN
  DATE_FORMAT(NOW(), '%Y-%m-01')  -- First day of the
current month
  AND  DATE_ADD(DATE_FORMAT(NOW(),  '%Y-%m-01'),
INTERVAL 3 MONTH) -- Last day of the current quarter
GROUP BY ProductID;
```

In this chapter, we explored how to work with **date and time** data in SQL:

- We learned key **SQL date functions** like DATE, NOW(), DATE_ADD(), and DATE_SUB().
- We covered how to **extract specific components** from dates (e.g., year, month, day).
- We applied these functions to a **real-world example**: analyzing monthly sales trends by grouping data based on year and month.
- We discussed how to use **advanced date operations** to calculate and filter dates relative to the current date.

In **Chapter 12**, we will dive into **window functions**—a powerful SQL feature for performing advanced calculations across a set of rows while retaining the individual row's identity.

CHAPTER 12: WINDOW FUNCTIONS FOR ADVANCED ANALYSIS

Introduction to Window Functions

Window functions (also called **analytic functions**) are powerful tools in SQL that allow you to perform calculations across a set of rows that are related to the current row, without collapsing the result set. Unlike aggregate functions like SUM() or AVG() that return a single value for a group of rows, window functions operate on a "window" of data and return a value for each row, providing more flexibility and advanced analysis capabilities.

These functions are extremely useful when you need to perform complex calculations like:

- **Running totals** or **cumulative sums**
- **Moving averages** for time series data
- **Ranking** of values based on certain criteria
- **Lead and lag** calculations for comparing data across different rows

In this chapter, we will cover some of the most common and useful window functions:

- **ROW_NUMBER**
- **RANK**
- **DENSE_RANK**
- **NTILE**
- **LEAD** and **LAG**

We will also walk through a **real-world example** of using window functions to calculate running totals of sales for each product over time.

1. Key Window Functions

Here are the core window functions you'll encounter in SQL:

1. **ROW_NUMBER()**

   o Assigns a unique number to each row within a result set. The numbering is based on the specified ORDER BY clause.

   o **Example**:

   sql

   ```
   SELECT ProductID, SaleDate, SaleAmount,
       ROW_NUMBER() OVER (ORDER BY SaleDate DESC) AS RowNum
   FROM Sales;
   ```

Result: Each row will get a unique row number, ordered by SaleDate in descending order.

2. **RANK()**

   o Ranks rows within a partition of the result set. If two rows have the same value, they will receive the same rank, and the next rank will be skipped (i.e., "gaps" in the ranks).

   o **Example**:

   sql

   SELECT ProductID, SaleAmount,
        RANK() OVER (ORDER BY SaleAmount DESC) AS Rank
   FROM Sales;

   Result: Products with higher sales amounts will have a lower rank number (1 is the highest).

3. **DENSE_RANK()**

   o Similar to RANK(), but does not skip ranks. If two rows have the same value, they will receive the same rank, but the next rank will continue sequentially (no gaps).

   o **Example**:

sql

SELECT ProductID, SaleAmount,

DENSE_RANK() OVER (ORDER BY SaleAmount DESC) AS DenseRank
FROM Sales;

Result: This will rank products with no gaps in rank numbers, even if two products have the same sales amount.

4. **NTILE()**

   o Divides the result set into a specified number of **equal** parts and assigns a bucket number to each row. The number of parts is determined by the argument passed to NTILE().

   o **Example**:

   sql

   SELECT ProductID, SaleAmount,

   NTILE(4) OVER (ORDER BY SaleAmount DESC) AS Quartile
   FROM Sales;

Result: The products will be divided into 4 quartiles based on sales amount, with each quartile representing 25% of the data.

5. **LEAD() and LAG()**

   o These functions allow you to access data from the next or previous row within the result set, without needing a self-join. LEAD() returns the value of a row after the current row, while LAG() returns the value of a row before the current row.

   o **LEAD():**

   sql

   ```
   SELECT ProductID, SaleDate, SaleAmount,
       LEAD(SaleAmount, 1) OVER (PARTITION
   BY ProductID ORDER BY SaleDate) AS NextSale
   FROM Sales;
   ```

   Result: For each product, the NextSale column will show the sales amount from the next sale transaction based on SaleDate.

   o **LAG():**

   sql

```
SELECT ProductID, SaleDate, SaleAmount,
    LAG(SaleAmount, 1) OVER (PARTITION BY
ProductID ORDER BY SaleDate) AS PrevSale
FROM Sales;
```

Result: For each product, the PrevSale column will show the sales amount from the previous sale transaction.

2. Using Window Functions for Advanced Calculations

The real power of window functions is revealed when you apply them to real-world data for advanced analysis. Let's go over some use cases that demonstrate how you can leverage these functions.

Running Totals and Cumulative Sums

A common use case for window functions is calculating **running totals**. For example, you might want to calculate the cumulative sales for each product over time. By using SUM() as an aggregate function in combination with a window function like ROWS BETWEEN UNBOUNDED PRECEDING AND CURRENT ROW, you can accumulate values over a time period.

Example:

Let's say we have a Sales table, and we want to calculate the cumulative sales for each product over time:

sql

```
SELECT
    ProductID,
    SaleDate,
    SaleAmount,
    SUM(SaleAmount) OVER (PARTITION BY ProductID
ORDER BY SaleDate ROWS BETWEEN UNBOUNDED
PRECEDING AND CURRENT ROW) AS RunningTotal
FROM Sales
ORDER BY ProductID, SaleDate;
```

Explanation:

- SUM(SaleAmount): Sums the sales amounts.
- PARTITION BY ProductID: Ensures that the cumulative sum is calculated separately for each product.
- ORDER BY SaleDate: Orders the rows by SaleDate for each product.
- ROWS BETWEEN UNBOUNDED PRECEDING AND CURRENT ROW: Defines the window frame, which includes all rows from the beginning of the partition to the current row.

Result:

ProductID SaleDate   SaleAmount RunningTotal

ProductID	SaleDate	SaleAmount	RunningTotal
1	2023-01-01	100	100
1	2023-01-02	200	300
1	2023-01-03	150	450
2	2023-01-01	250	250
2	2023-01-02	300	550
2	2023-01-03	100	650

The RunningTotal column shows the cumulative sales for each product, updated as we move through the rows.

Moving Averages

A **moving average** helps smooth out fluctuations in time series data and can reveal underlying trends. You can calculate a moving average using the AVG() function in combination with a window function like ROWS BETWEEN.

For example, let's calculate a **7-day moving average** of sales for each product:

sql

```
SELECT
    ProductID,
```

SaleDate,

SaleAmount,

AVG(SaleAmount) OVER (PARTITION BY ProductID ORDER BY SaleDate ROWS BETWEEN 6 PRECEDING AND CURRENT ROW) AS MovingAvg7Days
FROM Sales
ORDER BY ProductID, SaleDate;

Explanation:

- AVG(SaleAmount): Calculates the average of sales amounts.
- ROWS BETWEEN 6 PRECEDING AND CURRENT ROW: This defines the window to include the current row and the previous 6 rows (i.e., the past 7 days for each product).

Result:

ProductID	SaleDate	SaleAmount	MovingAvg7Days
1	2023-01-01	100	100
1	2023-01-02	200	150
1	2023-01-03	150	150
2	2023-01-01	250	250

ProductID SaleDate   SaleAmount MovingAvg7Days

| 2 | 2023-01-02 | 300 | 275 |

| 2 | 2023-01-03 | 100 | 216.67 |

This query calculates the average sales for each product over a 7-day period, smoothing out fluctuations in daily sales.

3. Real-World Example: Rank-Based Analysis

Another powerful application of window functions is for **ranking**. You may want to rank products based on their sales amount, or rank customers by the total amount they've spent. This is useful for identifying top performers or outliers in your data.

Example:

Let's rank products by total sales, and assign ranks to them. Products with equal sales will receive the same rank.

sql

```
SELECT
    ProductID,
    SUM(SaleAmount) AS TotalSales,
    RANK() OVER (ORDER BY SUM(SaleAmount) DESC) AS
SalesRank
FROM Sales
GROUP BY ProductID
```

ORDER BY SalesRank;

Explanation:

- RANK() OVER (ORDER BY SUM(SaleAmount) DESC): Ranks the products by total sales, with the highest sales getting the rank of 1.
- SUM(SaleAmount): Aggregates sales for each product.

Result:

ProductID TotalSales SalesRank

ProductID	TotalSales	SalesRank
1	1500	1
2	1200	2
3	1000	3

In this chapter, we:

- Introduced **window functions** such as ROW_NUMBER(), RANK(), DENSE_RANK(), NTILE(), and LEAD()/LAG().
- Explored how to use window functions for **advanced analyses** like **running totals**, **moving averages**, and **rank-based analysis**.

- Walked through real-world examples of calculating **cumulative sales** and **moving averages** for product sales over time.

In **Chapter 13**, we will explore **SQL optimization techniques**, focusing on how to improve query performance when working with large datasets.

CHAPTER 13: DATA TRANSFORMATION TECHNIQUES IN SQL

Introduction to Data Transformation

Data transformation refers to the process of converting data from its raw form into a format suitable for analysis or reporting. In the context of SQL, this involves using various functions to manipulate, clean, and structure data. Data transformation techniques are vital for preparing datasets that are inconsistent, incomplete, or not in the desired format for analysis.

In this chapter, we'll focus on:

- Using SQL functions to **transform data** (e.g., CONCAT, SUBSTRING, REPLACE).
- Performing **data type conversions** to ensure compatibility.
- **Formatting results** for better readability or consistency.
- Real-world examples of **normalizing and cleaning data**, such as phone numbers or email addresses, to prepare them for analysis.

1. SQL Functions for Data Transformation

SQL offers a variety of built-in functions to manipulate string, numeric, and date data types. These functions are essential for cleaning and formatting data before performing analysis.

String Functions for Data Transformation

1. **CONCAT()**

    o The CONCAT() function combines two or more strings into one.

    o **Syntax**:

    sql

    CONCAT(string1, string2, ..., stringN)

    o **Example**:

    sql

    SELECT CONCAT(FirstName, ' ', LastName) AS FullName
    FROM Employees;

    This query combines FirstName and LastName columns into a single column FullName.

2. **SUBSTRING()**

○ The SUBSTRING() function extracts a part of a string, starting at a specified position.

○ **Syntax**:

sql

SUBSTRING(string, start_position, length)

○ **Example**:

sql

SELECT SUBSTRING(PhoneNumber, 1, 3) AS AreaCode
FROM Contacts;

This query extracts the first three characters of the PhoneNumber column (usually the area code).

3. **REPLACE()**

○ The REPLACE() function allows you to substitute all occurrences of a substring with another substring.

○ **Syntax**:

sql

REPLACE(string, old_substring, new_substring)

o **Example**:

sql

SELECT REPLACE(EmailAddress, 'example.com', 'newdomain.com') AS UpdatedEmail
FROM Users;

This query updates all email addresses by replacing example.com with newdomain.com.

4. **TRIM()**
   o The TRIM() function removes leading and trailing spaces from a string.
   o **Syntax**:

   sql

   TRIM([LEADING | TRAILING | BOTH] trim_character FROM string)

   o **Example**:

   sql

   SELECT TRIM(BOTH ' ' FROM CustomerName) AS CleanedName

FROM Customers;

This query removes extra spaces from the CustomerName field.

5. **UPPER() and LOWER()**

  o These functions convert strings to upper or lower case, respectively.

  o **Syntax**:

  sql

  UPPER(string)
  LOWER(string)

  o **Example**:

  sql

  SELECT UPPER(EmailAddress) AS UpperEmail FROM Users;

  This query converts email addresses to uppercase.

6. **LEFT() and RIGHT()**

o These functions allow you to extract a specified number of characters from the left or right of a string.

o **Syntax**:

sql

LEFT(string, number_of_characters)
RIGHT(string, number_of_characters)

o **Example**:

sql

SELECT LEFT(PhoneNumber, 3) AS AreaCode,
RIGHT(PhoneNumber, 4) AS Last4Digits
FROM Contacts;

This query extracts the area code and the last four digits of the phone number.

Numeric Functions for Data Transformation

1. **ROUND()**

o The ROUND() function rounds numeric values to a specified number of decimal places.

o **Syntax**:

sql

ROUND(number, decimal_places)

- **Example**:

sql

SELECT ROUND(SaleAmount, 2) AS RoundedSale FROM Sales;

This query rounds the SaleAmount to two decimal places.

2. **CAST() and CONVERT()**
   - These functions convert one data type to another. CAST() is ANSI-standard, while CONVERT() is specific to certain SQL dialects like SQL Server.
   - **Syntax (CAST)**:

   sql

   CAST(expression AS data_type)

   - **Syntax (CONVERT)**:

   sql

CONVERT(data_type, expression)

o **Example (CAST)**:

sql

SELECT CAST(SaleAmount AS DECIMAL(10, 2)) AS FormattedSale
FROM Sales;

This query converts SaleAmount to a decimal with two decimal places.

2. Data Type Conversions and Formatting Results

Proper **data type conversions** are essential when dealing with inconsistent data. SQL provides several functions to ensure that your data is in the correct format before analysis or reporting.

Converting Dates and Timestamps

In SQL, dates and times are often stored as DATE, DATETIME, or TIMESTAMP data types. You might need to transform or format them to suit specific requirements.

1. **DATE_FORMAT() (MySQL) or TO_CHAR() (PostgreSQL/Oracle)**

o These functions allow you to format dates into readable strings.

o **Example (MySQL):**

sql

```
SELECT DATE_FORMAT(OrderDate, '%Y-%m-%d') AS FormattedDate
FROM Orders;
```

This query formats the OrderDate column into the YYYY-MM-DD format.

2. **DATE_TRUNC() (PostgreSQL)**

o The DATE_TRUNC() function truncates a timestamp to the specified level (e.g., year, month).

o **Example (PostgreSQL):**

sql

```
SELECT DATE_TRUNC('month', OrderDate) AS MonthStart
FROM Orders;
```

This query truncates the OrderDate to the start of the month.

3. Real-World Example: Normalizing and Cleaning Data

A common task for data analysts is to **clean and normalize** data before analysis. For example, phone numbers and email addresses often need formatting to ensure consistency.

Normalizing Phone Numbers

Phone numbers may be stored in various formats, but for consistency, you may want to standardize them into a specific format (e.g., (XXX) XXX-XXXX).

Example:

Let's say phone numbers are stored in the format XXX-XXX-XXXX or X(XXX)XXX-XXXX, and we want to standardize them.

sql

```
SELECT
    PhoneNumber,
    REPLACE(REPLACE(PhoneNumber, '-', ''), '(', '') AS
CleanedPhoneNumber
FROM Contacts;
```

This query first removes hyphens and parentheses, resulting in a cleaned phone number without any formatting. You could then use CONCAT() to add the desired formatting:

sql

SELECT

PhoneNumber,

CONCAT('(', SUBSTRING(CleanedPhoneNumber, 1, 3), ') ',

SUBSTRING(CleanedPhoneNumber, 4, 3), '-',

SUBSTRING(CleanedPhoneNumber, 7, 4)) AS

FormattedPhoneNumber

FROM Contacts;

Cleaning Email Addresses

Email addresses often contain unwanted spaces, inconsistent capitalization, or invalid characters. Here's how to clean them up.

1. **Remove leading/trailing spaces**:

sql

```
SELECT TRIM(EmailAddress) AS CleanedEmail
FROM Users;
```

2. **Convert email addresses to lowercase**:

sql

```
SELECT LOWER(EmailAddress) AS CleanedEmail
FROM Users;
```

3. **Remove invalid characters (e.g., spaces, commas)**:

sql

```
SELECT REPLACE(REPLACE(EmailAddress, ' ', ''), ',', '')
AS CleanedEmail
FROM Users;
```

By applying these transformations, you ensure that email addresses are clean, properly formatted, and consistent for further analysis or reporting.

In this chapter, we:

- Explored common **SQL string functions** (CONCAT, SUBSTRING, REPLACE) for transforming and cleaning data.
- Discussed **numeric transformations** with functions like ROUND(), CAST(), and CONVERT().
- Covered techniques for **data type conversions** and formatting results to make data suitable for analysis.
- Walked through a **real-world example** of normalizing phone numbers and cleaning email addresses.

In **Chapter 14**, we will dive into **data cleansing strategies** to handle missing or inconsistent data, an essential step in any data analyst's workflow.

CHAPTER 14: HANDLING NULL VALUES

Introduction to NULL in SQL

In SQL, **NULL** represents the absence of a value or the unknown. It is different from an empty string, zero, or any other value. NULL indicates that no data has been provided for a specific field. Handling NULL values is crucial in data analysis because they can distort results if not addressed correctly.

In this chapter, we will explore:

- The concept of **NULL** values in SQL.
- How to **filter** NULL values using IS NULL and IS NOT NULL.
- Techniques to **replace** NULL values with meaningful substitutes (e.g., default values or calculated replacements).
- Real-world examples of handling NULL values in customer profiles or sales transactions.

1. Understanding NULL Values

NULL in SQL is used to represent missing, undefined, or unknown data. It is a placeholder that differs from an empty string (") or zero (0). Here's a quick comparison:

- **NULL**: No data provided.
- **Empty String (")**: A value exists, but it is an empty string.
- **Zero (0)**: A numeric value, indicating zero.

Because NULL is neither a value nor an empty space, it requires special handling in SQL queries to avoid incorrect analysis or unexpected results.

Example: Consider a database with customer information, and one of the fields, PhoneNumber, is sometimes missing. If a customer does not have a phone number, that field will be NULL.

2. Filtering NULL Values

SQL provides ways to filter records with NULL values using the IS NULL and IS NOT NULL operators. These operators are essential for identifying rows where a value is missing or verifying that a field is populated.

Using IS NULL

- The IS NULL operator checks if a value in a column is NULL.
- **Syntax**:

sql

```
SELECT column_name
FROM table_name
WHERE column_name IS NULL;
```

- **Example**: Retrieve customers who have not provided a phone number.

sql

```
SELECT CustomerID, CustomerName, PhoneNumber
FROM Customers
WHERE PhoneNumber IS NULL;
```
This query will return all customers with a NULL value in the PhoneNumber field.

Using IS NOT NULL

- The IS NOT NULL operator checks if a value in a column is not NULL.
- **Syntax**:

sql

```
SELECT column_name
FROM table_name
```

WHERE column_name IS NOT NULL;

- **Example**: Retrieve customers who have a phone number listed.

sql

SELECT CustomerID, CustomerName, PhoneNumber
FROM Customers
WHERE PhoneNumber IS NOT NULL;
This query will return all customers with a non-NULL value in the PhoneNumber field.

3. Replacing NULL Values

Sometimes, NULL values need to be replaced with a meaningful value, especially for analysis or reporting purposes. For example, when handling customer data, a missing phone number might be replaced with a placeholder like "Not Provided," or a sales transaction with no value might be replaced with zero.

Using COALESCE()

The COALESCE() function returns the first non-NULL value from a list of arguments. This is particularly useful for replacing NULL values with a default value or calculated replacement.

- **Syntax**:

sql

COALESCE(expression1, expression2, ..., expressionN)

- **Example**: Replace NULL phone numbers with the text "Not Provided."

sql

SELECT   CustomerID,   CustomerName,
COALESCE(PhoneNumber,   'Not   Provided')   AS
PhoneNumber
FROM Customers;

In this query, if PhoneNumber is NULL, the string "Not Provided" is returned instead.

Using IFNULL() (MySQL) / NVL() (Oracle)

- MySQL provides the IFNULL() function, while Oracle and SQL Server offer NVL(). Both of these work similarly to COALESCE(), but only accept two arguments: the expression to check and the value to replace NULL.
- **Syntax (MySQL)**:

sql

IFNULL(expression, replacement_value)

- **Example**:

sql

SELECT CustomerID, CustomerName, IFNULL(PhoneNumber, 'Not Provided') AS PhoneNumber FROM Customers;
If PhoneNumber is NULL, this will replace it with "Not Provided".

Using CASE Statement for Conditional Replacements

Another option for replacing NULL values is using the CASE statement, which provides more flexibility for complex conditional logic.

- **Syntax**:

sql

CASE
  WHEN column_name IS NULL THEN replacement_value
  ELSE column_name
END

- **Example**:

sql

```
SELECT CustomerID, CustomerName,
    CASE
        WHEN PhoneNumber IS NULL THEN 'Not
Provided'
        ELSE PhoneNumber
    END AS PhoneNumber
FROM Customers;
```

This query checks if the PhoneNumber is NULL and replaces it with "Not Provided" when it is.

Using NULLIF()

- The NULLIF() function returns NULL if the two expressions are equal, otherwise it returns the first expression. While not commonly used for replacing NULLs, it can be useful in some specific cases.
- **Syntax**:

sql

```
NULLIF(expression1, expression2)
```

- **Example**:

sql

```
SELECT          CustomerID,          CustomerName,
NULLIF(PhoneNumber, '0000000000') AS PhoneNumber
FROM Customers;
```

This query replaces PhoneNumber with NULL if the value is '0000000000'.

4. Real-World Example: Handling Missing Data in Customer Profiles or Sales Transactions

Handling Missing Customer Data

Customer profiles often contain missing information. For example, let's say some customers have not provided an email address or phone number. We need to ensure that these NULL values are handled properly before performing any analysis or reporting.

1. **Identify customers with missing phone numbers**:

   sql

   ```
   SELECT CustomerID, CustomerName, PhoneNumber
   FROM Customers
   WHERE PhoneNumber IS NULL;
   ```

2. **Replace NULL phone numbers with a placeholder**:

   sql

```
SELECT          CustomerID,          CustomerName,
COALESCE(PhoneNumber,   'Not   Provided')   AS
PhoneNumber
FROM Customers;
```

3. **Replace NULL email addresses with a default email**:

sql

```
SELECT CustomerID, CustomerName,
    COALESCE(EmailAddress,  'noemail@example.com')
AS EmailAddress
FROM Customers;
```

Handling Missing Sales Transactions

Sales transactions might also have missing values. For instance, a transaction without a sale amount could be marked as NULL. If the NULL value represents a canceled or incomplete sale, you might want to replace it with zero to maintain consistency.

1. **Identify transactions with missing sales amounts**:

sql

```
SELECT TransactionID, ProductID, SaleAmount
FROM SalesTransactions
WHERE SaleAmount IS NULL;
```

2. **Replace NULL sale amounts with zero**:

sql

```
SELECT TransactionID, ProductID,
    COALESCE(SaleAmount, 0) AS SaleAmount
FROM SalesTransactions;
```

In this chapter, we:

- Explored the concept of **NULL values** in SQL and their implications in data analysis.
- Learned how to **filter** NULL values using IS NULL and IS NOT NULL.
- Discussed various methods to **replace** NULL values, including COALESCE(), IFNULL(), and the CASE statement.
- Walked through **real-world examples** of handling missing data in customer profiles and sales transactions.

In **Chapter 15**, we will focus on **SQL data cleansing techniques**, exploring how to deal with duplicates, inconsistent formats, and other common data issues.

CHAPTER 15: DATA NORMALIZATION AND DENORMALIZATION

Introduction to Data Normalization and Denormalization

Data normalization and denormalization are two fundamental techniques used in relational databases to manage the structure and efficiency of your data. Both processes aim to optimize how data is stored, accessed, and queried, but they serve different purposes and have trade-offs that impact performance and usability.

In this chapter, we will:

- Explore the concepts of **normalization** and **denormalization**.
- Understand the advantages and disadvantages of each approach.

- Apply normalization and denormalization in real-world scenarios, focusing on designing a sales database.

1. What is Data Normalization?

Normalization is the process of organizing a relational database to reduce data redundancy (repetitive data) and improve data integrity. The goal is to divide large tables into smaller, more manageable ones, each representing a single entity or concept. This process minimizes the chances of data anomalies and ensures that each piece of information is stored only once.

Normalization involves splitting a database into multiple tables and using **foreign keys** to maintain relationships between them. The most common levels of normalization are known as **normal forms**, which are a set of rules aimed at reducing redundancy.

Normal Forms (NF)

1. **First Normal Form (1NF)**: A table is in 1NF if it only contains atomic (indivisible) values. This means each column must contain only one value, and each row must be unique.
   - Example: A customer table should have only one phone number per record. A list of phone numbers in one cell would violate 1NF.
2. **Second Normal Form (2NF)**: A table is in 2NF if it is in 1NF and every non-key column is fully functionally

dependent on the primary key. This eliminates partial dependencies, where a column depends only on a part of the primary key.

- o Example: In a table of order details, the product name should not be stored with each order; instead, it should be stored in a separate product table and referenced by a product ID.

3. **Third Normal Form (3NF)**: A table is in 3NF if it is in 2NF and has no transitive dependencies. In other words, non-key columns should not depend on other non-key columns.

- o Example: A customer table should store only the customer's address and not their city and state directly if they are already stored in a separate address table.

Advantages of Normalization:

- **Data Integrity**: Reduces redundancy and the chances of inconsistent data.
- **Efficient Updates**: Modifications are centralized, so there is no need to update multiple rows with the same data.
- **Storage Efficiency**: Reduces the overall storage needed by eliminating duplicate data.

Disadvantages of Normalization:

- **Complexity**: Queries become more complex as data is spread across multiple tables.
- **Performance**: Can reduce performance in read-heavy systems due to the need for more joins between tables.

2. What is Data Denormalization?

Denormalization is the process of combining normalized tables back into fewer, larger tables to improve query performance, especially in read-heavy applications. While normalization reduces redundancy, denormalization intentionally introduces some redundancy to simplify and speed up queries.

Denormalization often involves creating a table that contains pre-joined or aggregated data, so queries do not require as many joins, which can be costly in terms of performance.

When to Denormalize:

Denormalization is particularly useful in scenarios where:

- **Performance is critical** (e.g., in reporting or data analytics applications).
- **Read operations** are far more frequent than write operations.
- **Query simplicity** is more important than storage efficiency.

Advantages of Denormalization:

- **Faster Queries**: Fewer joins can lead to faster read operations, especially for large datasets.
- **Simplified Queries**: Queries become simpler and more intuitive because the data is often stored in fewer tables.

Disadvantages of Denormalization:

- **Redundancy**: Introduces redundancy into the database, which can lead to inconsistency if updates are not handled properly.
- **Increased Storage**: Storing the same data in multiple places increases storage requirements.
- **More Complex Updates**: Since data is duplicated, updates must be applied to all instances of the redundant data.

3. Real-World Example: Designing a Sales Database

Let's walk through an example of designing a sales database for an e-commerce platform and see how both normalization and denormalization play out.

Sales Database Requirements:

- The database needs to store information about **customers**, **products**, **orders**, and **transactions**.
- We want to track **order details**, such as the products ordered, quantities, and prices.

- The database should also store **sales data** over time to perform reporting and analysis (e.g., total sales per region, per product, per time period).

Normalized Design (3NF)

To minimize redundancy and ensure data integrity, we can normalize the database to **3NF**.

1. **Customers Table**: Stores customer information.

   sql

   ```
   CREATE TABLE Customers (
       CustomerID INT PRIMARY KEY,
       CustomerName VARCHAR(255),
       Email VARCHAR(255),
       PhoneNumber VARCHAR(50),
       AddressID INT
   );
   ```

2. **Products Table**: Stores product details.

   sql

   ```
   CREATE TABLE Products (
       ProductID INT PRIMARY KEY,
       ProductName VARCHAR(255),
   ```

```
CategoryID INT,
Price DECIMAL(10, 2)
);
```

3. **Orders Table**: Stores order details, referencing the customer who placed the order.

sql

```
CREATE TABLE Orders (
    OrderID INT PRIMARY KEY,
    CustomerID INT,
    OrderDate DATE,
    FOREIGN KEY (CustomerID) REFERENCES Customers(CustomerID)
);
```

4. **OrderDetails Table**: Stores the products in each order. This is where we store many-to-many relationships.

sql

```
CREATE TABLE OrderDetails (
    OrderDetailID INT PRIMARY KEY,
    OrderID INT,
    ProductID INT,
    Quantity INT,
```

TotalPrice DECIMAL(10, 2),

FOREIGN KEY (OrderID) REFERENCES Orders(OrderID),

FOREIGN KEY (ProductID) REFERENCES Products(ProductID)

);

5. **Regions Table**: Stores region information for analysis.

sql

```sql
CREATE TABLE Regions (
    RegionID INT PRIMARY KEY,
    RegionName VARCHAR(255)
);
```

Denormalized Design

In a denormalized design, we might combine the Orders and OrderDetails tables into a single table to speed up queries.

1. **SalesReport Table**: Combines customer, product, and order details into a single table for easier reporting.

sql

```sql
CREATE TABLE SalesReport (
    SalesReportID INT PRIMARY KEY,
```

```
        OrderID INT,

        CustomerID INT,

        CustomerName VARCHAR(255),

        ProductID INT,

        ProductName VARCHAR(255),

        Quantity INT,

        TotalPrice DECIMAL(10, 2),

        OrderDate DATE,

        RegionName VARCHAR(255)

    );
```

This denormalized table includes **customer** and **region** information directly in the sales data, making reporting queries faster. For example, a query to get total sales by region can be simplified, as no joins are required.

Example Query: Total Sales by Region (Denormalized)

sql

```
SELECT RegionName, SUM(TotalPrice) AS TotalSales
FROM SalesReport
GROUP BY RegionName;
```

4. When to Choose Normalization vs. Denormalization

- **Normalization** is ideal when data integrity and minimizing redundancy are the primary concerns. It is best used in transactional systems where updates, inserts, and deletes are frequent and need to be consistent across the database.

- **Denormalization** is ideal for **analytical** databases or reporting systems where read performance and query simplicity are prioritized. It is best used in situations where complex joins would slow down performance and the data does not change as often.

In this chapter, we explored:

- The concepts of **normalization** and **denormalization**, including their benefits and drawbacks.
- How **normalization** reduces redundancy and ensures data integrity by dividing a database into smaller, more manageable tables.
- How **denormalization** sacrifices some data integrity to improve query performance by reducing the number of joins required.
- A **real-world example** of designing a sales database and how both normalization and denormalization impact its structure and performance.

In **Chapter 16**, we will dive into **advanced SQL joins** and explore techniques for merging complex datasets to derive insights across multiple dimensions.

CHAPTER 16: CREATING AND MODIFYING TABLES

Introduction to SQL Table Management

In this chapter, we'll explore how to create and modify tables in SQL, which are fundamental tasks for managing the structure of your database. Understanding these commands allows data analysts to effectively design, update, and refine their databases to meet evolving data requirements.

We will:

- Learn how to use **CREATE**, **ALTER**, and **DROP** commands.
- Understand how to modify the structure of existing tables (e.g., adding or removing columns, changing data types).
- Walk through a real-world example of creating and adjusting tables for a customer database.

1. Creating Tables with SQL

The **CREATE TABLE** command is used to define a new table in a database. It specifies the table's name, columns, and the type of data each column will hold. Additionally, you can define primary keys, foreign keys, and constraints to maintain data integrity.

Basic Syntax for Creating a Table:

sql

```
CREATE TABLE table_name (
    column_name data_type [constraint],
    column_name data_type [constraint],
    ...
);
```

- **table_name**: The name of the table you want to create.
- **column_name**: The name of each column in the table.
- **data_type**: The type of data (e.g., INT, VARCHAR, DATE).

- **constraint**: Constraints can include things like PRIMARY KEY, NOT NULL, UNIQUE, etc.

Example: Creating a Customer Table

Let's say we need to create a Customers table to store customer details for an e-commerce site.

sql

```
CREATE TABLE Customers (
    CustomerID INT PRIMARY KEY,          -- Unique identifier for each customer
    FirstName VARCHAR(50) NOT NULL,      -- Customer's first name
    LastName VARCHAR(50) NOT NULL,       -- Customer's last name
    Email VARCHAR(100) UNIQUE,           -- Customer's email, must be unique
    PhoneNumber VARCHAR(15),             -- Customer's phone number (optional)
    DateOfBirth DATE,                    -- Customer's date of birth
    Address VARCHAR(255)                 -- Customer's address
);
```

In this example:

- We've defined a **CustomerID** as the primary key to uniquely identify each customer.

- **FirstName**, **LastName**, and **Email** are required fields (NOT NULL).

- **Email** has a UNIQUE constraint, ensuring that no two customers can have the same email.

2. Modifying Tables with ALTER

The **ALTER TABLE** command is used to modify an existing table's structure. You can use it to add, delete, or modify columns, change data types, and even add constraints.

Common ALTER Commands:

- **Add a column**:

sql

```
ALTER TABLE table_name ADD column_name data_type;
```

- **Drop a column**:

sql

```
ALTER TABLE table_name DROP COLUMN column_name;
```

- **Modify a column's data type**:

sql

ALTER TABLE table_name MODIFY COLUMN column_name new_data_type;

- **Rename a column** (varies by database, e.g., in MySQL):

sql

ALTER TABLE table_name CHANGE old_column_name new_column_name new_data_type;

Example: Adding a New Column to the Customers Table

Let's say you need to add a column to the Customers table to store the customer's loyalty program membership status:

sql

ALTER TABLE Customers ADD LoyaltyStatus VARCHAR(20) DEFAULT 'Bronze';

This command:

- Adds a new column **LoyaltyStatus** to the Customers table.
- The default value for new records is set to 'Bronze'.

Example: Changing Data Type of a Column

Suppose the PhoneNumber column needs to store international numbers and needs to be updated to support a larger character limit. You could modify it as follows:

sql

ALTER TABLE Customers MODIFY COLUMN PhoneNumber VARCHAR(20);

This command increases the length of the **PhoneNumber** column from VARCHAR(15) to VARCHAR(20).

Example: Dropping a Column

If you want to remove a column that is no longer needed (for example, the Address column), you can drop it:

sql

ALTER TABLE Customers DROP COLUMN Address;

This will remove the **Address** column from the table entirely.

3. Dropping Tables with DROP

The **DROP TABLE** command is used to permanently delete a table and all of its data from the database. This operation cannot be undone, so be cautious when using it.

Syntax for Dropping a Table:

sql

DROP TABLE table_name;

Example: Dropping the Customers Table

If you need to remove the entire Customers table, use:

sql

DROP TABLE Customers;

This will remove the table and its data from the database. If there are any foreign key constraints referencing this table in other tables, you may need to drop those constraints first.

4. Real-World Example: Adjusting a Customer Database

Let's walk through a real-world example of how we would create and modify a customer database for an e-commerce business.

Step 1: Creating the Initial Table

Start by creating the **Customers** table with basic information, such as CustomerID, FirstName, and LastName.

sql

```
CREATE TABLE Customers (
    CustomerID INT PRIMARY KEY,
    FirstName VARCHAR(50),
    LastName VARCHAR(50),
    Email VARCHAR(100) UNIQUE
);
```

Step 2: Adding New Columns for More Detailed Information

After collecting feedback, the company decides to include **phone numbers**, **addresses**, and **birthday** information for customer profiling. We will add these new columns.

sql

```
ALTER TABLE Customers
ADD PhoneNumber VARCHAR(15),
    Address VARCHAR(255),
    DateOfBirth DATE;
```

Step 3: Changing Column Data Types

Later, the company decides to allow for international phone numbers, so the PhoneNumber column must support a longer length. We will modify it:

sql

```
ALTER TABLE Customers MODIFY COLUMN PhoneNumber VARCHAR(20);
```

Step 4: Dropping Unnecessary Columns

After a system upgrade, the company no longer needs to store the customer's **Address** information in this table, so we will drop it.

sql

ALTER TABLE Customers DROP COLUMN Address;

Step 5: Dropping the Table (Optional)

If the company decides to abandon the entire customer management system, they may choose to drop the **Customers** table altogether:

sql

DROP TABLE Customers;

In this chapter, we covered:

- **Creating tables** using the CREATE TABLE statement, defining the structure and data types for each column.
- **Modifying tables** with ALTER TABLE to add, delete, or modify columns and data types, and using constraints for data integrity.
- **Dropping tables** with the DROP TABLE command to permanently remove a table and its data.
- A **real-world example** of creating, modifying, and adjusting a customer database to accommodate evolving business needs.

In **Chapter 17**, we will explore **advanced indexing techniques** to improve the speed of data retrieval in large datasets and enhance the overall performance of our SQL queries.

CHAPTER 17: INDEXING AND QUERY OPTIMIZATION

Introduction to Indexing and Query Performance

As data grows in volume, the need for efficient querying becomes critical. SQL databases provide tools to speed up data retrieval, and one of the most powerful tools for this is **indexing**. Just like the index at the back of a book helps you quickly find information, indexes in a database make data retrieval faster and more efficient by allowing SQL queries to find and retrieve data without having to scan every row in a table.

In this chapter, we will:

- Explore **what indexes are** and how they work.
- Learn **best practices** for creating and managing indexes.
- Examine **real-world examples** where indexing improves query performance, such as speeding up queries on a large sales table.

1. Understanding Indexes in SQL

An **index** in a database is a data structure that improves the speed of data retrieval operations. Indexes are typically created on columns that are frequently used in **WHERE, JOIN, ORDER BY**, or **GROUP BY** clauses. They allow the database to find rows more quickly, avoiding the need to scan the entire table.

How Indexes Work:

- When you create an index on a table, the database builds a separate data structure that contains the indexed column values along with a reference (pointer) to the corresponding rows in the table.
- When a query is executed that involves the indexed column, the database can use the index to quickly locate the relevant rows rather than scanning the whole table, which speeds up the query.

Example of an Index:

If you have a **Customers** table and frequently query by the Email column, you can create an index on the Email column to speed up searches:

sql

CREATE INDEX idx_email ON Customers(Email);

In this example, idx_email is the name of the index, and it will help optimize queries that filter or search for customers by email.

2. Types of Indexes

Different types of indexes can be used in SQL, depending on the use case and the database system:

- **Single-column Index**: An index created on a single column of a table.
  - Example:

    sql

    CREATE INDEX idx_lastname ON Customers(LastName);

    This index helps speed up queries that filter by LastName.

- **Composite Index**: An index created on multiple columns. It is used when queries filter on several columns simultaneously.

  o Example:

  sql

  CREATE   INDEX   idx_name_email   ON Customers(FirstName, LastName, Email);

  This index is useful if you frequently query by a combination of FirstName, LastName, and Email.

- **Unique Index**: Ensures that no two rows in the table have the same value for the indexed columns. This is automatically created when a PRIMARY KEY or UNIQUE constraint is defined.

  o Example:

  sql

  CREATE UNIQUE INDEX idx_unique_email ON Customers(Email);

- **Full-text Index**: A specialized index used for full-text searches (common in content-rich databases).

  o Example (for MySQL):

sql

CREATE   FULLTEXT   INDEX
idx_fulltext_description ON Products(Description);

3. Best Practices for Indexing

While indexes can significantly improve query performance, over-indexing can hurt performance due to the overhead of maintaining these indexes, especially when data is inserted, updated, or deleted. Here are some best practices to follow:

Best Practices:

1. **Index Columns Used in WHERE, JOIN, and ORDER BY Clauses**:
   - o If you frequently filter data using a specific column (e.g., WHERE column_name = value), it's a good idea to create an index on that column.
   - o Example: If you frequently query sales data by ProductID, create an index on ProductID.

sql

CREATE INDEX idx_productid ON Sales(ProductID);

2. **Use Composite Indexes for Multi-column Queries**:

- o If you regularly filter or join on multiple columns, a composite index can help speed up those queries.
- o Example: If you often search for transactions by both CustomerID and OrderDate, a composite index might be beneficial.

sql

```
CREATE INDEX idx_customer_orderdate ON Orders(CustomerID, OrderDate);
```

3. **Avoid Over-Indexing**:
   - o Each index slows down **INSERT, UPDATE,** and **DELETE** operations because the database needs to update the index each time data is modified. Therefore, index only those columns that are frequently used in queries.

4. **Use the Right Type of Index**:
   - o For simple lookups or range queries, a basic index is usually sufficient.
   - o For full-text searches or complex pattern matching, consider using **full-text** indexes.

5. **Monitor and Drop Unused Indexes**:
   - o Over time, certain indexes may become obsolete as the use cases change. Regularly review and drop

indexes that aren't used by your queries to improve database performance.

sql

DROP INDEX idx_unused_column ON table_name;

4. Query Optimization Tips

While indexing plays a huge role in speeding up queries, there are other techniques that can further improve the performance of your SQL queries:

1. **Avoid SELECT * (Wildcard Selects)**:
   o Instead of using SELECT *, explicitly specify the columns you need. This reduces the amount of data the database has to retrieve.

sql

SELECT FirstName, LastName FROM Customers WHERE Email = 'example@example.com';

2. **Use EXPLAIN to Analyze Queries**:
   o The EXPLAIN keyword can help you understand how the database is executing a query. It shows the execution plan, and you can use it to optimize your queries.

sql

```
EXPLAIN SELECT FirstName, LastName FROM
Customers WHERE Email = 'example@example.com';
```

3. **Use Proper Join Types**:
   - Use INNER JOIN when you only need rows that exist in both tables, and use LEFT JOIN when you need all rows from the left table, even if there's no match in the right table. Avoid unnecessary RIGHT JOIN or FULL JOIN when possible.

4. **Limit the Number of Rows**:
   - Use LIMIT to restrict the number of rows returned, especially when dealing with large datasets.

sql

```
SELECT * FROM Sales ORDER BY SaleDate DESC
LIMIT 100;
```

5. **Optimize Subqueries**:
   - Subqueries can sometimes be slow. Consider converting them to **JOINs** or using **CTEs** (Common Table Expressions) for better performance.

5. Real-World Example: Indexing a Large Sales Table

Let's consider a **Sales** table with millions of records, and we frequently run queries to analyze sales data. The queries often filter by ProductID, CustomerID, and SaleDate. To improve the speed of these queries, we can create indexes on these columns.

Creating Indexes:

1. **Index on ProductID**: Since we often query sales data by product, we'll create an index on the ProductID column.

   sql

   CREATE INDEX idx_productid ON Sales(ProductID);

2. **Composite Index on CustomerID and SaleDate**: If we regularly analyze sales by specific customers and their purchases over time, a composite index can help speed up queries that filter on both CustomerID and SaleDate.

   sql

   CREATE INDEX idx_customer_saledate ON Sales(CustomerID, SaleDate);

Query Optimization:

- **Before indexing**, a query like:

sql

SELECT ProductID, SUM(Amount) FROM Sales WHERE SaleDate BETWEEN '2023-01-01' AND '2023-12-31' GROUP BY ProductID;

might take a long time to execute because the database has to scan all rows in the Sales table.

- **After indexing**, the database will use the idx_productid and idx_customer_saledate indexes to quickly find the relevant data, speeding up the query execution time significantly.

In this chapter, we:

- Explored the concept of **indexing** and how it helps improve the performance of SQL queries.
- Discussed **best practices** for creating effective indexes and managing them to ensure optimal performance.
- Walked through a **real-world example** of indexing a large sales table to speed up query execution.

By understanding and applying indexing and optimization techniques, data analysts can handle large datasets efficiently, making their SQL queries faster and more responsive.

In **Chapter 18**, we'll dive into **advanced techniques for managing large datasets** and look at performance tuning strategies beyond indexing, such as partitioning and query rewriting.

CHAPTER 18: HANDLING LARGE DATASETS WITH SQL

Introduction

In the real world, many data analysts and data scientists work with large datasets that can be difficult to manage, query, and analyze.

As databases grow in size, querying them efficiently becomes more challenging. Handling large datasets efficiently is essential to maintaining high-performance queries, ensuring that data can be processed and analyzed in a reasonable time frame.

This chapter will focus on techniques and strategies for working with large datasets in SQL, including:

- **Partitioning**: Dividing large datasets into smaller, more manageable pieces.
- **Batch Processing**: Processing data in smaller chunks to avoid performance bottlenecks.
- **Performance Considerations**: Optimizing queries to handle massive datasets efficiently.

We will also look at a **real-world example** of how partitioning can be used to analyze **global sales data**, making queries more efficient.

1. Techniques for Working with Large Datasets

Handling large datasets in SQL involves more than just basic querying. It requires a set of techniques that help optimize performance, reduce processing time, and ensure that the system can handle the volume of data effectively. Below are key techniques used when working with large datasets.

Partitioning

Partitioning is the process of dividing a large table into smaller, more manageable pieces called **partitions**. Each partition is treated as a separate unit, but they are still part of the same table. This can improve query performance by limiting the amount of data that needs to be scanned in a query.

There are several ways to partition data:

- **Range Partitioning**: Dividing data based on a range of values, such as date ranges.
- **List Partitioning**: Dividing data based on a predefined list of values, such as regions or product categories.
- **Hash Partitioning**: Dividing data based on a hash function, which can be useful when no logical grouping exists.

Example: Range Partitioning

Let's say you have a **Sales** table with millions of rows, and you often run queries that filter by **SaleDate**. To improve performance, you can partition the table by **SaleDate** so that each partition holds a specific range of dates (e.g., one partition for each year).

sql

```
CREATE TABLE Sales (
    SaleID INT,
    CustomerID INT,
    ProductID INT,
```

```
    Amount DECIMAL(10, 2),
    SaleDate DATE
)
PARTITION BY RANGE (YEAR(SaleDate)) (
    PARTITION p_2020 VALUES LESS THAN (2021),
    PARTITION p_2021 VALUES LESS THAN (2022),
    PARTITION p_2022 VALUES LESS THAN (2023)
);
```

In this example, data from the **Sales** table is partitioned into three partitions, one for each year. When querying for sales in 2021, the query will only scan the **p_2021** partition, making it much faster.

Batch Processing

For extremely large datasets, processing all the data at once may be inefficient or infeasible due to memory constraints. **Batch processing** is the practice of breaking up large datasets into smaller, manageable chunks or batches for processing over time.

Example: Batch Querying with OFFSET and LIMIT

When dealing with a large result set, you can use OFFSET and LIMIT to retrieve data in smaller chunks. This allows you to process the data incrementally, reducing the load on the database and preventing timeouts.

sql

```
SELECT * FROM Sales
```

ORDER BY SaleDate

LIMIT 1000 OFFSET 0; -- First 1000 records

SELECT * FROM Sales

ORDER BY SaleDate

LIMIT 1000 OFFSET 1000; -- Next 1000 records

In this example, you retrieve 1000 records at a time from the Sales table. You can adjust the OFFSET value to get subsequent batches, making it easier to process large datasets in stages.

Sharding

Sharding is a method used to distribute data across multiple databases or servers. This is typically used when a single server or database cannot handle the size or load of the data. Sharding helps by distributing the data across different machines, allowing for parallel processing and improving query performance.

While sharding can be complex and requires good infrastructure, it can provide a significant performance boost when working with truly massive datasets.

2. *Performance Considerations When Querying Massive Datasets*

When querying large datasets, the complexity and performance of your SQL queries can be significantly impacted. It is important to consider the following strategies to improve query performance when working with massive datasets:

1. Query Optimization

- **Use Indexes**: As discussed in Chapter 17, indexes can drastically improve query performance. Ensure that appropriate indexes are in place, particularly on columns used in WHERE, JOIN, ORDER BY, or GROUP BY clauses.

- **Limit the Result Set**: Avoid fetching unnecessary data by using the LIMIT clause to return only the rows you need, especially when dealing with very large tables.

- ****Avoid SELECT *****: Instead of using SELECT *, specify only the columns needed in the query. This reduces the amount of data retrieved and speeds up the query.

2. Query Refactoring

Sometimes, a complex query can be optimized by breaking it into smaller, simpler queries. Instead of running a long, complicated query, consider breaking it into subqueries or temporary tables that can be processed more efficiently.

For example, if you need to calculate the total sales per product across multiple years, you might start by creating intermediate results that can be aggregated in a final step.

3. Partition Pruning

When partitioning tables, **partition pruning** is a technique that ensures the query only scans relevant partitions. In databases with partitioned tables, the query optimizer will typically skip over partitions that do not match the query's filtering criteria, which improves performance.

For example, in the range-partitioned Sales table mentioned earlier, if you query for sales in 2021, only the **p_2021** partition will be scanned.

sql

```
SELECT ProductID, SUM(Amount)
FROM Sales
WHERE SaleDate BETWEEN '2021-01-01' AND '2021-12-31'
GROUP BY ProductID;
```

This query will only access the data in the p_2021 partition, making it much more efficient.

4. Database Configuration and Hardware Considerations

- **Increase Memory and CPU Resources**: For very large datasets, having adequate memory (RAM) and CPU capacity can significantly improve query performance.
- **Use Parallel Query Execution**: Some databases, such as PostgreSQL, can execute queries in parallel across multiple cores or nodes, which can speed up processing on large datasets.

3. Real-World Example: Analyzing Global Sales Data Efficiently Using Partitions

Let's consider a global **Sales** table with millions of records. The dataset includes information about sales transactions across various regions, product categories, and time periods. Analyzing the entire dataset for trends such as monthly sales performance or regional comparisons can be time-consuming without proper optimization.

Step 1: Partitioning the Sales Data

To improve query performance, we can partition the **Sales** table based on the **SaleDate** (using range partitioning). This will allow us to quickly filter by year or month.

sql

```
CREATE TABLE Sales (
    SaleID INT,
    CustomerID INT,
    ProductID INT,
    Amount DECIMAL(10, 2),
    SaleDate DATE,
    Region VARCHAR(50)
)
PARTITION BY RANGE (YEAR(SaleDate)) (
    PARTITION p_2020 VALUES LESS THAN (2021),
    PARTITION p_2021 VALUES LESS THAN (2022),
```

PARTITION p_2022 VALUES LESS THAN (2023)
);

Step 2: Efficient Querying with Partition Pruning

Now, when we query sales data for a specific year, the database will only access the relevant partition, speeding up the query.

For example, if we want to analyze **sales in 2021**, the query will look only at the p_2021 partition:

sql

```
SELECT Region, SUM(Amount)
FROM Sales
WHERE SaleDate BETWEEN '2021-01-01' AND '2021-12-31'
GROUP BY Region;
```

Because the database uses **partition pruning**, it will only scan the p_2021 partition, making this query much faster than if it had to scan the entire dataset.

Step 3: Batch Processing for Large Query Results

If we need to analyze all sales data for multiple regions over multiple years, we can break the analysis into smaller chunks using **batch processing**. For example, instead of querying all data at once, we can retrieve and process data year by year or region by region.

sql

```
SELECT Region, SUM(Amount)
FROM Sales
WHERE SaleDate BETWEEN '2020-01-01' AND '2020-12-31'
GROUP BY Region
LIMIT 1000 OFFSET 0;
```

This process can be repeated with different OFFSET values to get additional batches of results.

In this chapter, we discussed techniques for handling large datasets efficiently in SQL, focusing on **partitioning** and **batch processing** as key strategies. We also covered:

- **Partitioning** for managing large tables by dividing them into smaller, more manageable pieces.
- **Batch processing** to incrementally process data in smaller chunks.
- **Performance considerations** such as query optimization, partition pruning, and hardware improvements.

By applying these strategies, you can optimize SQL queries and ensure that your data analysis remains efficient, even when working with massive datasets. In the next chapter, we'll dive deeper into **database maintenance** and how to keep your databases optimized as they grow in size and complexity.

CHAPTER 19: TRANSACTIONS AND DATA INTEGRITY

Introduction

In any real-world database system, ensuring data consistency and reliability is crucial. This becomes especially important when dealing with multiple users or complex data manipulations, such as updating inventory, processing payments, or recording sales transactions. **Transactions** play a key role in ensuring that operations on the database maintain data integrity.

A **transaction** is a sequence of one or more SQL operations executed as a single unit. Transactions allow you to group related queries together so that they can either all succeed or all fail, ensuring the database remains in a consistent state.

In this chapter, we'll explore the concepts of:

- **SQL transactions**: How to manage and control transactions.
- **ACID properties**: How transactions maintain the consistency and integrity of your data.
- **Real-world example**: Managing inventory data with transactions to prevent errors and maintain consistency.

1. Introduction to SQL Transactions

A **transaction** in SQL is a logical unit of work that is executed in a sequence. A transaction can consist of multiple SQL statements (such as INSERT, UPDATE, or DELETE), and it must adhere to the **ACID** properties to ensure that the database remains in a valid state.

The fundamental operations that manage transactions are:

- **BEGIN TRANSACTION**: Marks the start of a transaction. All operations following this statement are part of the transaction.
- **COMMIT**: Saves the changes made during the transaction to the database permanently.
- **ROLLBACK**: Reverts all changes made during the transaction, undoing any updates or inserts performed within the transaction.

Example: Basic Transaction Syntax

sql

```
-- Start the transaction
BEGIN;


-- Insert a new product into the inventory
INSERT INTO Products (ProductName, Quantity, Price)
VALUES ('Laptop', 50, 1200.00);


-- Update the inventory to reflect a stock deduction (sale)
UPDATE Products
SET Quantity = Quantity - 10
WHERE ProductID = 1;


-- Commit the transaction, making changes permanent
COMMIT;
```

In the above example, we first start a transaction with BEGIN. Then, we perform an INSERT and an UPDATE. Finally, we COMMIT the transaction, ensuring the changes are saved to the database.

If an error occurs before we commit the transaction (e.g., a stock update fails due to insufficient quantity), we can use ROLLBACK to undo all changes made during the transaction, ensuring the database is not left in an inconsistent state.

2. ACID Properties

The **ACID** properties ensure that database transactions are processed reliably and help maintain data integrity, even in the face of system failures or errors. These properties are:

- **Atomicity**: Ensures that all operations within a transaction are completed successfully. If any operation fails, the entire transaction is rolled back, leaving the database unchanged.

  Example: If we were transferring funds from one bank account to another and the system crashed after deducting money but before adding it to the other account, atomicity ensures the transaction is rolled back, so the money is not lost.

- **Consistency**: Guarantees that a transaction brings the database from one valid state to another. Any changes made within the transaction must follow all predefined rules and constraints, such as foreign keys, unique constraints, etc.

Example: If you're transferring money from one account to another, consistency ensures that the total balance of both accounts remains correct after the transaction.

- **Isolation**: Ensures that the operations of one transaction are isolated from the operations of other concurrent transactions. This prevents transactions from interfering with each other.

  Example: If two users are updating the same product's price at the same time, isolation ensures that the updates are performed in a way that prevents data corruption or inconsistencies.

- **Durability**: Once a transaction has been committed, its changes are permanent and will survive any system crashes or failures. The data is written to disk and cannot be lost.

  Example: After a successful purchase transaction in an e-commerce system, durability ensures that the purchase details are stored in the database and will not be lost if the system crashes immediately after the transaction.

3. Ensuring Data Consistency with Transactions

In many real-world applications, multiple operations must be performed together, and these operations need to be either fully completed or fully undone to maintain consistency. Transactions provide a way to guarantee this.

Example: Managing Inventory Data with Transactions

Consider an inventory management system in which products are sold, and their quantities must be updated in the database. Let's say a customer orders a product, and the inventory must be decremented, the order must be recorded, and payment needs to be processed.

Without transactions, if the system crashes after updating the inventory but before completing the order, the database could be left in an inconsistent state, where the inventory is updated but no order was actually recorded. Transactions help avoid such problems by ensuring that all operations are completed together or not at all.

Here's an example of how you would manage inventory and sales using transactions:

sql

```
-- Start the transaction
BEGIN;
```

```sql
-- Check if the product is available in stock
SELECT Quantity FROM Products WHERE ProductID = 101;


-- Assume we check the quantity, and it's sufficient


-- Update the inventory to deduct the sold quantity
UPDATE Products
SET Quantity = Quantity - 1
WHERE ProductID = 101;


-- Record the sale in the Sales table
INSERT INTO Sales (ProductID, CustomerID, Quantity, SaleDate)
VALUES (101, 15, 1, NOW());


-- If all operations succeed, commit the transaction
COMMIT;
```

If any of the steps fail (for example, if the inventory is insufficient or the sale cannot be recorded), you can use ROLLBACK to undo all changes made during the transaction, preserving the integrity of the data.

sql


```sql
-- If there is an error at any point, you can roll back the changes
```

ROLLBACK;

In this example:

- **Atomicity** ensures that both the UPDATE and INSERT are either both committed or both rolled back.
- **Consistency** ensures that the update to the inventory and the recording of the sale maintain the validity of the database (e.g., no product is sold without being in stock).
- **Isolation** ensures that no other transaction can interfere with this process while it's running.
- **Durability** ensures that once the transaction is committed, the changes to both the inventory and the sales records are permanent.

4. Real-World Example: Preventing Errors in Inventory Management

Imagine a situation where multiple employees are processing sales transactions concurrently. Without proper use of transactions, there could be race conditions where two employees attempt to sell the last available item of a product simultaneously. This could result in overselling and data inconsistencies.

Let's say two employees are selling the last unit of a particular product at the same time:

1. **Employee 1** checks the inventory, sees that one unit is available, and starts processing a sale.

2. **Employee 2** checks the inventory at the same time, also sees that one unit is available, and starts processing another sale.

3. Both employees try to update the inventory at the same time, causing an inconsistency.

By using transactions, these problems can be avoided. If the inventory check and update are part of a transaction, and the system detects an issue (e.g., insufficient stock), it will automatically roll back one of the transactions, preventing the overselling.

Here's an example of how we can ensure that only one transaction successfully updates the inventory:

sql

```
BEGIN;

-- Try to reduce the quantity, but if the quantity is zero, fail the transaction
UPDATE Products
SET Quantity = Quantity - 1
WHERE ProductID = 101 AND Quantity > 0;

-- If no rows were affected (because Quantity was 0), rollback the transaction
```

```
IF ROW_COUNT() = 0 THEN
   ROLLBACK;
   RAISE ERROR 'Insufficient stock';
END IF;
```

```
-- Otherwise, proceed with recording the sale
INSERT INTO Sales (ProductID, CustomerID, Quantity, SaleDate)
VALUES (101, 15, 1, NOW());
```

```
-- Commit the transaction if successful
COMMIT;
```

In this example, the **UPDATE** statement checks that the product has a positive quantity before attempting to decrement it. If the product's quantity is zero or negative, the transaction will be rolled back, and the sale will not be recorded, preventing overselling.

In this chapter, we covered the importance of transactions for ensuring data integrity and consistency in SQL databases. Transactions help group related SQL operations together and provide guarantees about the reliability and correctness of those operations through the **ACID properties** (Atomicity, Consistency, Isolation, and Durability).

Key takeaways:

- Transactions allow multiple operations to be executed as a single unit of work.

- ACID properties ensure that the database remains in a consistent and reliable state.

- Transactions help prevent errors in critical systems, such as inventory management, by guaranteeing that operations are fully completed or fully rolled back.

In the next chapter, we'll explore how to handle advanced database topics like **database constraints**, which further ensure the integrity and validity of your data.

CHAPTER 20: WORKING WITH TEMPORARY TABLES AND VIEWS

Introduction

In the world of data analysis, there are times when we need to break down complex queries or store intermediate results for later use. **Temporary tables** and **views** are powerful tools that help simplify and optimize queries, making it easier to manage complex datasets and perform repeated analyses without redundant code. These tools are particularly useful when you're working with large datasets or need to aggregate and analyze data multiple times throughout your analysis.

In this chapter, we'll cover:

- **Temporary Tables**: How to create and use temporary tables to store intermediate results.
- **Views**: How to create reusable virtual tables that represent queries or aggregations.
- **Real-world Example**: Creating a view for monthly sales summary reports.

1. Temporary Tables: What and Why?

A **temporary table** is a table that exists only for the duration of a session or transaction. It is used to store temporary data that is needed for intermediate calculations or for simplifying complex queries. Temporary tables are particularly useful when you're working with subqueries or need to store intermediate results between multiple steps of a query.

Why Use Temporary Tables?

- Simplify complex queries by breaking them down into smaller parts.
- Improve query performance by storing intermediate results that can be reused.
- Ensure that temporary data doesn't persist beyond the session or transaction, keeping your database clean.

Creating and Using Temporary Tables

Temporary tables are created using the CREATE TEMPORARY TABLE statement. These tables behave like regular tables, but they are dropped automatically when the session or connection is closed.

Basic Syntax:

sql

-- Create a temporary table

```
CREATE TEMPORARY TABLE temp_sales_summary AS
SELECT ProductID, SUM(Quantity) AS TotalSold, AVG(Price)
AS AvgPrice
FROM Sales
GROUP BY ProductID;


-- Query the temporary table
SELECT * FROM temp_sales_summary;


-- Drop the temporary table (optional, as it will be dropped
automatically at the end of the session)
DROP TEMPORARY TABLE temp_sales_summary;
```

In the example above:

- We first create a **temporary table** temp_sales_summary that stores the total quantity sold and the average price for each product.
- We then query the temporary table as if it were a regular table.
- Finally, we drop the temporary table, although it will automatically be dropped when the session ends.

2. Views: Simplifying Repetitive Queries

A **view** is a virtual table based on the result of a SELECT query. Unlike temporary tables, views are persistent and stored in the database schema. Views don't store data themselves; instead, they store the SQL query that generates the data when queried. Views are useful for encapsulating complex logic and presenting simplified results, making it easier to reuse and maintain queries without rewriting them.

Why Use Views?

- **Reusability**: Define complex queries once, and reuse them as if they were simple tables.
- **Simplicity**: Hide the complexity of the query logic from the end user or analyst.
- **Performance**: In some cases, views can optimize queries by materializing frequently-used aggregations or joins, depending on the database engine's capabilities.

Creating and Using Views

A view is created using the CREATE VIEW statement. Once created, you can query a view just like a regular table.

Basic Syntax:

sql

```
-- Create a view for monthly sales summary
CREATE VIEW monthly_sales_summary AS
SELECT
    YEAR(SaleDate) AS SaleYear,
```

```
MONTH(SaleDate) AS SaleMonth,
SUM(Quantity) AS TotalSold,
AVG(Price) AS AvgPrice,
SUM(Quantity * Price) AS TotalRevenue
FROM Sales
GROUP BY YEAR(SaleDate), MONTH(SaleDate);

-- Query the view to get monthly sales data
SELECT * FROM monthly_sales_summary
WHERE SaleYear = 2023 AND SaleMonth = 10;
```

In the example above:

- We create a view called monthly_sales_summary that summarizes the total sales, average price, and total revenue for each month.
- We can then query the view just like a regular table to fetch the monthly summary, without needing to write the aggregation query each time.

Benefits of Views

- **Code Reusability**: The monthly_sales_summary view can be used by multiple analysts or tools without rewriting the query each time.

- **Encapsulation**: The complex aggregation logic is encapsulated in the view, simplifying the querying process for users who don't need to understand the underlying SQL.
- **Security**: Views can limit the data exposed to users by restricting access to only certain columns or aggregations, providing an additional layer of security.

3. Temporary Tables vs Views

While both temporary tables and views simplify complex queries, they serve different purposes and have different use cases.

- **Temporary Tables**:
  - Exist only for the duration of a session or transaction.
  - Are used to store intermediate results that can be used in multiple queries within the session.
  - Can be modified (inserted into, updated, deleted).
  - More flexible in terms of data manipulation but less permanent.
- **Views**:
  - Are stored in the database schema and persist beyond the session.
  - Represent a static query and cannot be modified directly (they are read-only).

o Provide a convenient way to encapsulate logic for reuse.

o More suited for repeated querying and simplifying complex logic.

Which to Use?

- Use **temporary tables** when you need to store intermediate data for the current session, or if you need to perform operations like INSERT, UPDATE, or DELETE on the data.

- Use **views** when you want to simplify repeated queries or encapsulate complex logic that you want to reuse across multiple sessions or users.

4. Real-World Example: Creating a View for Monthly Sales Summary

Let's say you're an analyst at a retail company, and you need to generate monthly sales summary reports. Instead of writing the same aggregation query each time, you can create a view to simplify your work.

1. **Step 1**: Create the view to aggregate sales data by month.

sql

CREATE VIEW monthly_sales_summary AS

```sql
SELECT
    YEAR(SaleDate) AS SaleYear,
    MONTH(SaleDate) AS SaleMonth,
    SUM(Quantity) AS TotalSold,
    AVG(Price) AS AvgPrice,
    SUM(Quantity * Price) AS TotalRevenue
FROM Sales
GROUP BY YEAR(SaleDate), MONTH(SaleDate);
```

2. **Step 2**: Query the view to get the sales data for a specific month.

sql

```sql
SELECT * FROM monthly_sales_summary
WHERE SaleYear = 2023 AND SaleMonth = 10;
```

3. **Step 3**: If you need to see sales trends for multiple months, you can expand the query.

sql

```sql
SELECT SaleYear, SaleMonth, TotalSold, AvgPrice, TotalRevenue
FROM monthly_sales_summary
WHERE SaleYear = 2023
ORDER BY SaleMonth;
```

With this view, you no longer need to write the full aggregation query every time you need a monthly report. The view simplifies your work and ensures consistency across all reports.

In this chapter, we've explored how to work with **temporary tables** and **views** in SQL to simplify complex queries, improve efficiency, and create reusable data models for analysis. Here's a summary of the key takeaways:

- **Temporary Tables** are useful for storing intermediate results and simplifying complex queries within a session or transaction.
- **Views** are virtual tables that encapsulate complex logic, allowing you to reuse queries and simplify report generation.
- Both tools can improve performance, reduce redundancy, and enhance data analysis workflows, but they are used in different scenarios depending on the need for data manipulation or reusability.

In the next chapter, we'll dive into **transactions and data integrity**, exploring how to ensure your data remains consistent and reliable in a multi-user environment.

CHAPTER 21: FINANCIAL DATA ANALYSIS WITH SQL

Introduction

Financial data analysis is a critical part of decision-making in any business or investment context. Whether you're tracking revenue, managing budgets, forecasting growth, or analyzing market trends, SQL is an invaluable tool for organizing, querying, and interpreting financial data. By using SQL, analysts can query large datasets, perform aggregations, calculate financial ratios, and more. This chapter focuses on how to use SQL for financial data analysis, with practical examples to demonstrate its power in analyzing business performance.

In this chapter, we will:

- Explore common financial analysis tasks such as budgeting, forecasting, and trend analysis.
- Walk through a real-world example of analyzing quarterly revenue data to track business performance.

1. Financial Data Analysis Tasks in SQL

a. Budgeting and Forecasting:

- SQL can be used to track a company's budget and compare it to actual performance. Analysts often write queries that calculate variances between budgeted and actual figures and then visualize or report those variances for decision-makers.
- Forecasting involves using historical data to predict future trends, and SQL can play a role in preparing and cleaning this data for more advanced analysis, often combining SQL with other forecasting tools or machine learning models.

b. Trend Analysis:

- Trend analysis refers to examining financial data over time to identify patterns or movements. This could involve analyzing revenue growth, tracking expense categories, or identifying seasonality.

- SQL's GROUP BY, HAVING, and date-based functions can be used to segment data into time periods (months, quarters, years), calculate sums or averages, and help highlight trends.

2. Analyzing Quarterly Revenue Data: A Real-World Example

Let's assume you're working as a financial analyst at a company that tracks quarterly revenue. You've been tasked with analyzing the revenue trends and comparing them to the budgeted revenue.

Step 1: Set Up the Data

Imagine you have a table called Revenue in your SQL database with the following columns:

- Quarter: The fiscal quarter (e.g., Q1, Q2, Q3, Q4).
- Year: The year of the revenue data (e.g., 2023).
- ActualRevenue: The actual revenue for the quarter.
- BudgetedRevenue: The planned or forecasted revenue for the quarter.

Here's how the table might look:

Quarter	Year	ActualRevenue	BudgetedRevenue
Q1	2023	500,000	550,000
Q2	2023	600,000	580,000

Quarter	Year	ActualRevenue	BudgetedRevenue
Q3	2023	700,000	690,000
Q4	2023	650,000	660,000

Step 2: Write Basic SQL Queries for Analysis

We'll start with some basic SQL queries to calculate revenue performance for each quarter and year.

a. Total Revenue per Quarter

First, let's calculate the total actual and budgeted revenue for each quarter in 2023.

sql

```
SELECT Quarter,
     SUM(ActualRevenue) AS TotalActualRevenue,
     SUM(BudgetedRevenue) AS TotalBudgetedRevenue
FROM Revenue
WHERE Year = 2023
GROUP BY Quarter
ORDER BY Quarter;
```

Result:

Quarter TotalActualRevenue TotalBudgetedRevenue

Quarter	TotalActualRevenue	TotalBudgetedRevenue
Q1	500,000	550,000
Q2	600,000	580,000
Q3	700,000	690,000
Q4	650,000	660,000

This simple query provides a summary of the actual versus budgeted revenue for each quarter.

b. Calculating Variance Between Actual and Budgeted Revenue

Now, let's calculate the variance between the actual and budgeted revenue for each quarter.

sql

```sql
SELECT Quarter,
    (SUM(ActualRevenue)  -  SUM(BudgetedRevenue))  AS
RevenueVariance
FROM Revenue
WHERE Year = 2023
GROUP BY Quarter
ORDER BY Quarter;
```

Result:

Quarter RevenueVariance

Q1   -50,000

Q2   20,000

Q3   10,000

Q4   -10,000

In this case, the company underperformed in Q1 and Q4 but exceeded its budget in Q2 and Q3. These variances can be used to trigger further analysis or alert management to areas needing attention.

Step 3: Trend Analysis with SQL

Next, let's conduct a trend analysis to determine how the company's revenue is evolving over the quarters. We'll calculate the **quarter-over-quarter growth rate** for actual revenue.

Formula for Growth Rate:

Growth Rate=Current Quarter Revenue−Previous Quarter Revenue Previous Quarter Revenue×100\text{Growth   Rate}   = \frac{\text{Current Quarter Revenue} - \text{Previous Quarter Revenue}}{\text{Previous   Quarter   Revenue}}   \times 100Growth Rate=Previous Quarter RevenueCurrent Quarter Revenue−Previous Quarter Revenue×100

To calculate the growth rate for each quarter, we can use a **self-join** to compare each quarter's revenue with the previous quarter's revenue:

sql

```
SELECT r1.Quarter,
     r1.Year,
     r1.ActualRevenue AS CurrentRevenue,
     r2.ActualRevenue AS PreviousRevenue,
     ((r1.ActualRevenue - r2.ActualRevenue) / r2.ActualRevenue) * 100 AS GrowthRate
FROM Revenue r1
JOIN Revenue r2
  ON r1.Year = r2.Year
  AND r1.Quarter = CASE
            WHEN r2.Quarter = 'Q1' THEN 'Q4'
            WHEN r2.Quarter = 'Q2' THEN 'Q1'
            WHEN r2.Quarter = 'Q3' THEN 'Q2'
            WHEN r2.Quarter = 'Q4' THEN 'Q3'
          END
WHERE r1.Year = 2023
ORDER BY r1.Quarter;
```

Result:

Quarter	Year	CurrentRevenue	PreviousRevenue	GrowthRate
Q2	2023	600,000	500,000	20%
Q3	2023	700,000	600,000	16.67%
Q4	2023	650,000	700,000	-7.14%

From this analysis, we can see that revenue grew by 20% from Q1 to Q2, 16.67% from Q2 to Q3, but then declined by 7.14% from Q3 to Q4.

Step 4: Visualizing the Data

While SQL is powerful for performing calculations and aggregations, visualization tools can enhance your analysis. Most data visualization platforms (like Tableau, Power BI, or even Python with libraries such as Matplotlib and Seaborn) can connect to your SQL database and generate charts based on these results.

For instance:

- A **line chart** of actual revenue over the four quarters could help you visualize the trend.
- A **bar chart** comparing actual versus budgeted revenue can help identify underperforming or overperforming periods.

3. Real-World Applications of SQL in Financial Analysis

SQL plays a crucial role in the day-to-day tasks of financial analysts. Here are some other ways SQL is commonly used in financial analysis:

- **Budget Variance Analysis**: Tracking how actual performance compares to the forecasted or budgeted performance.
- **Cash Flow Management**: Analyzing inflows and outflows of cash, as well as forecasting cash needs.
- **Profitability Analysis**: Calculating and comparing profit margins for different products, regions, or time periods.
- **Financial Ratios**: Using SQL to calculate key financial ratios like Return on Investment (ROI), Return on Assets (ROA), or Gross Profit Margin.

In this chapter, we've explored how SQL can be used to analyze financial data by focusing on common tasks like budgeting, forecasting, and trend analysis. We've used **quarterly revenue data** as a case study to demonstrate key SQL techniques, including:

- Aggregation of data (SUM(), AVG()).
- Trend analysis with JOIN and calculations for growth rates.
- Analyzing variances between actual and budgeted values.

By mastering these SQL techniques, you can transform raw financial data into actionable insights that help businesses understand their performance, optimize operations, and make data-driven decisions. In the next chapter, we'll explore **marketing data analysis with SQL**, showing how to leverage SQL for customer segmentation and campaign performance analysis.

CHAPTER 22: CUSTOMER BEHAVIOR ANALYSIS WITH SQL

Introduction

Understanding customer behavior is a cornerstone of effective business strategy. By analyzing customer interactions, purchasing patterns, and retention rates, businesses can identify key drivers of loyalty, optimize marketing efforts, and reduce churn. SQL is an essential tool for this kind of analysis, as it allows you to extract meaningful insights from large datasets related to customer transactions, demographics, and engagement.

In this chapter, we will explore how to use SQL to:

- Analyze customer behavior through transaction data.
- Track customer churn and retention.
- Identify loyal customers based on purchasing frequency and recency.

We'll also walk through a real-world example of identifying the most loyal customers using purchasing frequency, which is a common task in customer behavior analysis.

---

1. Analyzing Customer Behavior with SQL

To understand customer behavior, we often rely on several key metrics:

- **Purchase Frequency**: How often a customer makes a purchase.

- **Recency**: How recently a customer made a purchase.

- **Monetary Value**: How much money a customer spends over a given time period.

- **Churn Rate**: The rate at which customers stop buying or leave a service.

- **Customer Retention**: The ability of a business to keep customers over time.

SQL helps analyze these metrics through aggregation, filtering, and advanced joins.

2. Key Metrics for Customer Behavior Analysis

Here are a few critical metrics for customer behavior analysis that you can calculate with SQL:

a. Purchase Frequency

- This metric indicates how frequently a customer makes a purchase within a specific period (e.g., monthly, quarterly, annually). A high frequency of purchases often indicates strong customer loyalty.

SQL Example:

sql

```
SELECT CustomerID, COUNT(OrderID) AS PurchaseFrequency
FROM Orders
```

GROUP BY CustomerID

ORDER BY PurchaseFrequency DESC;

This query counts the number of orders each customer made, helping identify customers with the highest purchase frequency.

b. Recency of Purchase

- Recency refers to how recently a customer has made a purchase. Recent customers are more likely to make future purchases, while those who haven't bought in a while might be at risk of churn.

SQL Example:

sql

SELECT CustomerID, MAX(OrderDate) AS LastPurchaseDate

FROM Orders

GROUP BY CustomerID

ORDER BY LastPurchaseDate DESC;

This query finds the last purchase date for each customer, which can be used to calculate recency.

c. Monetary Value

- The total monetary value of a customer's purchases is an indicator of their overall contribution to revenue. SQL can be used to aggregate sales data and calculate the total amount spent by each customer.

SQL Example:

sql

```
SELECT CustomerID, SUM(TotalAmount) AS TotalSpent
FROM Orders
GROUP BY CustomerID
ORDER BY TotalSpent DESC;
```

This query calculates the total amount spent by each customer across all their orders.

d. Customer Lifetime Value (CLV)

- CLV is the predicted net profit from the entire future relationship with a customer. It combines data on frequency, recency, and monetary value into one metric, often used for segmentation and targeting.

SQL Example:

sql

```
SELECT CustomerID,
    SUM(TotalAmount) AS TotalSpent,
    COUNT(OrderID) AS TotalPurchases,
```

DATEDIFF(CURRENT_DATE, MAX(OrderDate)) AS Recency

FROM Orders

GROUP BY CustomerID;

This query pulls together all relevant customer behavior data (total spent, number of orders, and recency) to calculate customer lifetime value in a simplified form.

3. Churn and Retention Analysis

a. Calculating Churn Rate

- Churn rate measures the percentage of customers who stop making purchases or cancel a service over a given period. By analyzing churn rates, businesses can identify whether they need to improve customer retention strategies.

SQL Example: To calculate churn, we might first identify customers who made a purchase in a given time frame and then track how many of them did not make any further purchases after that period.

sql

```
-- Find customers who made a purchase in the last 12 months
SELECT DISTINCT CustomerID
FROM Orders
```

```
WHERE    OrderDate    >    DATE_SUB(CURRENT_DATE,
INTERVAL 12 MONTH);
```

```
-- Find customers who made a purchase in the last 12 months but
not in the last 3 months
SELECT DISTINCT CustomerID
FROM Orders
WHERE    OrderDate    >    DATE_SUB(CURRENT_DATE,
INTERVAL 12 MONTH)
  AND CustomerID NOT IN (
    SELECT DISTINCT CustomerID
    FROM Orders
    WHERE    OrderDate    >    DATE_SUB(CURRENT_DATE,
INTERVAL 3 MONTH)
  );
```

This query identifies customers who made a purchase within the last 12 months but have since stopped purchasing for 3 months, indicating they may have churned.

b. Calculating Retention Rate

- Retention rate is the inverse of churn rate, tracking how many customers return to make a purchase after their first purchase.

SQL Example: To calculate retention rate, we can count how many customers who made a purchase in a specific period (e.g., 2023) made another purchase in a subsequent period.

sql

```
SELECT COUNT(DISTINCT o1.CustomerID) AS RetainedCustomers
FROM Orders o1
JOIN Orders o2 ON o1.CustomerID = o2.CustomerID
WHERE o1.OrderDate BETWEEN '2023-01-01' AND '2023-12-31'
  AND o2.OrderDate > '2023-12-31';
```

This query returns the number of customers who made purchases in 2023 and also made a subsequent purchase after 2023, indicating retention.

4. Identifying Loyal Customers

a. Loyalty Scoring

- Loyal customers are often those who purchase frequently, spend more, and have a recent purchase history. By combining these factors, we can create a **loyalty score** for each customer.

SQL Example: We can calculate a basic loyalty score by weighing factors like frequency, recency, and spending:

sql

```
SELECT CustomerID,
    COUNT(OrderID) AS PurchaseFrequency,
    MAX(OrderDate) AS LastPurchaseDate,
    SUM(TotalAmount) AS TotalSpent,
    DATEDIFF(CURRENT_DATE, MAX(OrderDate)) AS
Recency,
    (COUNT(OrderID) * 0.4 + SUM(TotalAmount) * 0.4 +
(DATEDIFF(CURRENT_DATE, MAX(OrderDate)) * 0.2)) AS
LoyaltyScore
FROM Orders
GROUP BY CustomerID
ORDER BY LoyaltyScore DESC;
```

In this query, we assign a weight to each metric (purchase frequency, spending, recency) to calculate a loyalty score. The higher the score, the more loyal the customer.

b. Filtering the Most Loyal Customers

Once the loyalty scores are calculated, you can filter out the most loyal customers, for example, by selecting the top 10% of customers.

sql

```
WITH Loyalty AS (
```

```
SELECT CustomerID,
    (COUNT(OrderID) * 0.4 + SUM(TotalAmount) * 0.4 +
(DATEDIFF(CURRENT_DATE, MAX(OrderDate)) * 0.2)) AS
LoyaltyScore
    FROM Orders
    GROUP BY CustomerID
)
SELECT CustomerID, LoyaltyScore
FROM Loyalty
WHERE LoyaltyScore > (SELECT PERCENTILE_CONT(0.9)
WITHIN GROUP (ORDER BY LoyaltyScore) FROM Loyalty);
```

This query filters out the top 10% most loyal customers based on the loyalty score.

5. Real-World Application: Analyzing Customer Loyalty

By identifying and analyzing customer behavior, businesses can design targeted retention campaigns, improve their product offerings, and create personalized marketing strategies. For instance, loyal customers can be rewarded with discounts or special promotions, while at-risk customers (those with low purchase frequency or high recency) can be targeted with re-engagement campaigns.

SQL is an incredibly powerful tool for analyzing customer behavior, churn, and retention. By using basic SQL functions and advanced techniques like joins, window functions, and subqueries, you can:

- Identify loyal customers based on purchasing frequency, recency, and spending.
- Calculate churn and retention rates to inform customer retention strategies.
- Gain actionable insights that help businesses improve customer engagement and profitability.

In the next chapter, we'll dive deeper into **marketing campaign analysis** with SQL, showing how to evaluate the effectiveness of different marketing strategies using customer data.

CHAPTER 23: SALES AND MARKETING ANALYSIS WITH SQL

Introduction

Sales and marketing are the lifeblood of any business, and understanding how to analyze the effectiveness of sales strategies and marketing campaigns is crucial for driving growth. By using SQL, data analysts can extract insights that guide decision-making, identify successful promotional strategies, and optimize marketing efforts for better ROI (Return on Investment).

In this chapter, we will cover how SQL can be used to:

- Analyze sales data to track performance.
- Evaluate the effectiveness of various marketing campaigns.
- Compare the impact of different promotional strategies on sales.

We will also walk through a real-world example of comparing the impact of different promotional strategies (e.g., discounts, seasonal offers, and email campaigns) on sales performance.

1. Analyzing Sales Data with SQL

Before we delve into marketing analysis, it's important to understand how to analyze basic sales data, which will form the foundation of any marketing analysis.

a. Sales Performance Metrics

Some of the key metrics you might analyze to assess sales performance include:

- **Total Sales**: Total revenue generated over a period.
- **Sales Growth**: The percentage change in sales compared to a previous period.
- **Sales by Product or Category**: Breakdown of sales by individual products or product categories.

SQL Example: To calculate the total sales and sales growth over two periods (e.g., Q1 vs. Q2):

sql

```
-- Total Sales in Q1
SELECT SUM(TotalAmount) AS Q1Sales
FROM Orders
WHERE OrderDate BETWEEN '2023-01-01' AND '2023-03-31';


-- Total Sales in Q2
SELECT SUM(TotalAmount) AS Q2Sales
FROM Orders
WHERE OrderDate BETWEEN '2023-04-01' AND '2023-06-30';


-- Sales Growth from Q1 to Q2
```

```
SELECT
   (SUM(CASE WHEN OrderDate BETWEEN '2023-04-01' AND
'2023-06-30' THEN TotalAmount ELSE 0 END) -
    SUM(CASE WHEN OrderDate BETWEEN '2023-01-01' AND
'2023-03-31' THEN TotalAmount ELSE 0 END)) /
    SUM(CASE WHEN OrderDate BETWEEN '2023-01-01' AND
'2023-03-31' THEN TotalAmount ELSE 0 END) * 100
   AS SalesGrowthPercentage
FROM Orders;
```

In this example, we calculate total sales in two quarters (Q1 and Q2) and then measure the sales growth between those periods.

2. Evaluating the Effectiveness of Marketing Campaigns

Marketing campaigns can take various forms—email promotions, social media ads, seasonal sales, etc. To evaluate the success of a marketing campaign, SQL helps to link sales data with marketing activities, usually by associating customers' orders with the campaign they responded to.

a. Key Metrics for Marketing Campaign Evaluation

- **Conversion Rate**: The percentage of customers who made a purchase after receiving or engaging with a marketing campaign.
- **Campaign Revenue**: The total revenue generated by a campaign.

- **Customer Acquisition Cost (CAC)**: The cost of acquiring a customer through a specific marketing campaign.
- **Return on Investment (ROI)**: The ratio of campaign revenue to the cost of the campaign.

SQL Example: Let's say you have a table Campaigns that tracks various marketing campaigns, and a Sales table that tracks customer orders. To calculate the effectiveness of a campaign:

sql

```
-- Calculate Campaign Revenue (for a specific campaign)
SELECT SUM(TotalAmount) AS CampaignRevenue
FROM Orders
WHERE CampaignID = 'SummerSale2023';


-- Calculate Conversion Rate for the campaign
SELECT
    (COUNT(DISTINCT CASE WHEN CampaignID =
'SummerSale2023' THEN OrderID END) /
    COUNT(DISTINCT CASE WHEN CampaignID =
'SummerSale2023' THEN CustomerID END)) * 100 AS
ConversionRate
FROM Orders;


-- Calculate ROI for the campaign
```

```
SELECT
    (SUM(TotalAmount) - CampaignCost) / CampaignCost AS ROI
FROM Orders
JOIN    Campaigns    ON    Orders.CampaignID    =
Campaigns.CampaignID
WHERE Campaigns.CampaignID = 'SummerSale2023';
```

In these queries:

- The **Campaign Revenue** is the total revenue generated by a specific campaign.
- The **Conversion Rate** measures how many customers who interacted with a campaign actually made a purchase.
- **ROI** measures the profitability of the campaign by comparing the revenue generated against the cost of running the campaign.

3. Comparing the Impact of Different Promotional Strategies

Businesses often run multiple promotional campaigns at the same time or sequentially. Analyzing the comparative effectiveness of these campaigns helps in deciding which strategies to pursue further. Let's say you want to compare the effectiveness of two types of promotions: **Discounts** and **Seasonal Offers**.

SQL Example: Here's how you can compare the sales impact of two different promotional strategies by analyzing the sales generated during each campaign period:

```sql
sql

-- Sales generated during Discount Promotion
SELECT SUM(TotalAmount) AS DiscountSales
FROM Orders
WHERE CampaignID = 'DiscountPromo' AND OrderDate
BETWEEN '2023-06-01' AND '2023-06-30';

-- Sales generated during Seasonal Offer Promotion
SELECT SUM(TotalAmount) AS SeasonalSales
FROM Orders
WHERE CampaignID = 'SeasonalOffer' AND OrderDate
BETWEEN '2023-06-01' AND '2023-06-30';

-- Compare the two promotional strategies (Discount vs. Seasonal Offer)
SELECT
    (SELECT SUM(TotalAmount) FROM Orders WHERE CampaignID = 'DiscountPromo' AND OrderDate BETWEEN '2023-06-01' AND '2023-06-30') AS DiscountSales,
    (SELECT SUM(TotalAmount) FROM Orders WHERE CampaignID = 'SeasonalOffer' AND OrderDate BETWEEN '2023-06-01' AND '2023-06-30') AS SeasonalSales,
```

(SELECT SUM(TotalAmount) FROM Orders WHERE CampaignID = 'DiscountPromo' AND OrderDate BETWEEN '2023-06-01' AND '2023-06-30') /

(SELECT SUM(TotalAmount) FROM Orders WHERE CampaignID = 'SeasonalOffer' AND OrderDate BETWEEN '2023-06-01' AND '2023-06-30') AS SalesComparison;

This query compares the sales generated by two campaigns (a Discount Promo and a Seasonal Offer) during the same period, giving you a clear view of which strategy had a bigger impact.

4. Analyzing Marketing Channels

To further optimize marketing efforts, it's crucial to understand which channels (e.g., email, social media, online ads) are most effective at driving sales. This can be achieved by linking campaign data to specific channels.

SQL Example: To measure how different marketing channels contribute to sales:

sql

```
-- Total sales by marketing channel
SELECT MarketingChannel, SUM(TotalAmount) AS TotalSales
FROM Orders
JOIN Campaigns ON Orders.CampaignID = Campaigns.CampaignID
GROUP BY MarketingChannel
```

ORDER BY TotalSales DESC;

This query aggregates the total sales by marketing channel, helping you determine which channels are most effective at generating revenue.

5. Real-World Application: Comparing Promotional Strategies

Let's put this into a more practical example. Imagine you work for an e-commerce business and your company recently ran two promotional campaigns: a **Discount Promotion** and a **Seasonal Sale**. The goal is to evaluate which strategy generated more sales and had the best ROI.

Using the queries above, you would first analyze the total sales and ROI for both campaigns. Then, based on the data, you can provide insights such as:

- Which campaign generated more revenue?
- Which strategy had a higher conversion rate (e.g., how many people who saw the campaign actually made a purchase)?
- Which campaign provided the best return on investment?

By conducting this analysis, your team can make data-driven decisions on which promotional strategies to invest more in or adjust for future campaigns.

Sales and marketing analysis using SQL is an essential skill for data analysts looking to measure the effectiveness of promotional campaigns. By using SQL to track sales data, evaluate campaign performance, and compare different strategies, businesses can make informed decisions that drive growth and profitability.

In the next chapter, we will explore **Customer Segmentation and Targeting** using SQL, where we'll look at how to segment customers based on various criteria and create targeted marketing strategies for each segment.

CHAPTER 24: FINAL PROJECT: END-TO-END DATA ANALYSIS WITH SQL

Introduction

The culmination of your journey through SQL for data analysis is this final project, where you will tie together everything you've learned from data collection, cleaning, and transformation, to complex analysis and deriving actionable insights. This chapter will guide you through an end-to-end project that mimics real-world scenarios, giving you the skills to tackle data analysis tasks effectively.

For this project, we'll use a **retail sales dataset**—which can represent a company's sales transactions over a period of time—and perform various analyses, from basic data cleaning and preparation to advanced analysis that drives business decisions.

By the end of this project, you'll have created a comprehensive SQL solution that answers key business questions, identifies trends, and provides actionable insights to improve business performance.

Project Overview: Analyzing Retail Company Sales Data

Imagine you are an analyst at a retail company that wants to understand its sales performance over the past year. The company has a large transactional database containing information such as:

- **Orders**: Information about each transaction, including order ID, customer, product, amount, and date.
- **Customers**: Data about customers, including demographics and purchase history.
- **Products**: Product details like category, price, and inventory levels.
- **Campaigns**: Details about marketing campaigns that may have affected sales.

Your task is to:

1. Clean and transform the raw data.
2. Perform a series of analyses to answer critical business questions.
3. Generate insights that can drive future business decisions.

Step 1: Data Collection and Setup

The first step in any data analysis project is to gather and prepare the data. For this project, you will:

1. **Set up a database**: Use an SQL-based tool (such as MySQL, PostgreSQL, or SQLite) to import the data into your local or cloud-based database.
2. **Inspect the data**: Understand the structure of the tables (Orders, Customers, Products, Campaigns) and examine the fields, data types, and relationships between them.

Example of setting up the tables:

sql

```
-- Creating a Customers table
CREATE TABLE Customers (
    CustomerID INT PRIMARY KEY,
    CustomerName VARCHAR(255),
    Gender VARCHAR(10),
    Age INT,
    Email VARCHAR(255),
    PhoneNumber VARCHAR(20),
    Address VARCHAR(255)
);

-- Creating an Orders table
CREATE TABLE Orders (
    OrderID INT PRIMARY KEY,
    CustomerID INT,
    ProductID INT,
    OrderDate DATE,
    TotalAmount DECIMAL(10, 2),
    CampaignID INT,
    FOREIGN KEY (CustomerID) REFERENCES Customers(CustomerID),
```

```
    FOREIGN       KEY       (ProductID)       REFERENCES
Products(ProductID)
);
```

```
-- Creating a Products table
CREATE TABLE Products (
    ProductID INT PRIMARY KEY,
    ProductName VARCHAR(255),
    Category VARCHAR(50),
    Price DECIMAL(10, 2),
    Inventory INT
);
```

```
-- Creating a Campaigns table
CREATE TABLE Campaigns (
    CampaignID INT PRIMARY KEY,
    CampaignName VARCHAR(255),
    StartDate DATE,
    EndDate DATE,
    Cost DECIMAL(10, 2)
);
```

Once your tables are set up, you'll need to import the data from CSV or other sources into these tables.

Step 2: Data Cleaning and Transformation

Before diving into analysis, the data needs to be cleaned. Common tasks include:

- **Handling missing values**: NULL values might exist in the dataset, especially in optional fields like customer contact info or product reviews.
- **Normalizing inconsistent data**: Data might need to be standardized (e.g., date formats, address formats).
- **Filtering irrelevant data**: Remove any rows that are outside the scope of analysis, such as incomplete transactions or duplicate orders.

Example of filtering out NULL values and fixing incorrect formats:

sql

```
-- Removing orders where total amount is NULL or zero
DELETE FROM Orders WHERE TotalAmount IS NULL OR
TotalAmount = 0;

-- Standardizing date formats (if needed)
UPDATE Orders SET OrderDate = STR_TO_DATE(OrderDate,
'%Y-%m-%d') WHERE OrderDate IS NOT NULL;
```

In this step, you'll also want to transform or aggregate data where necessary—for example, creating age groups for customers or categorizing products into broader types.

Step 3: Data Analysis

This is the most crucial step, where you apply SQL to answer business questions using the cleaned data.

Business Question 1: What were the total sales by product category?

To identify which product categories are performing best, you would aggregate sales data by category:

sql

```
SELECT p.Category, SUM(o.TotalAmount) AS TotalSales
FROM Orders o
JOIN Products p ON o.ProductID = p.ProductID
GROUP BY p.Category
ORDER BY TotalSales DESC;
```

This query will return a list of product categories and their corresponding sales, ordered by highest revenue.

Business Question 2: How did marketing campaigns impact sales?

To measure the effectiveness of marketing campaigns, we can compare sales during campaign periods versus non-campaign periods:

sql

```
-- Sales during a specific campaign
SELECT SUM(o.TotalAmount) AS CampaignSales
FROM Orders o
JOIN Campaigns c ON o.CampaignID = c.CampaignID
WHERE c.CampaignID = 1 AND o.OrderDate BETWEEN c.StartDate AND c.EndDate;


-- Sales outside of campaigns
SELECT SUM(o.TotalAmount) AS NonCampaignSales
FROM Orders o
WHERE o.CampaignID IS NULL OR o.OrderDate NOT BETWEEN '2023-06-01' AND '2023-06-30';
```

This analysis allows you to understand the impact of a specific campaign on sales compared to a baseline period without a campaign.

Business Question 3: What are the top-performing customers?

Identifying your most valuable customers can help in focusing marketing and retention efforts. This query calculates the total spend per customer:

sql

```
SELECT c.CustomerName, SUM(o.TotalAmount) AS TotalSpent
FROM Orders o
JOIN Customers c ON o.CustomerID = c.CustomerID
GROUP BY c.CustomerName
ORDER BY TotalSpent DESC
LIMIT 10;
```

This provides a list of the top 10 customers by total spend, which can be used for targeted marketing.

Step 4: Generating Actionable Insights

After performing the analysis, it's time to draw actionable insights that drive business decisions. For example:

- **Sales trends**: If certain product categories are underperforming, the company can focus on improving these areas or discontinue low-performing products.
- **Campaign effectiveness**: If certain campaigns yielded high sales, similar future campaigns can be modeled after them.
- **Customer segmentation**: By identifying top spenders, the business can create personalized marketing strategies or loyalty programs to retain these valuable customers.

Step 5: Reporting and Visualization

In the final stage, you'll want to present your findings in a way that's easy to digest for decision-makers. You could:

- **Create views**: Simplify complex queries by creating reusable views for reporting purposes.
- **Export results**: Use SQL queries to export data into CSV or Excel for further visualization in tools like Tableau, Power BI, or Excel.

Example of creating a view for sales performance:

sql

```
CREATE VIEW SalesPerformance AS
SELECT p.Category, SUM(o.TotalAmount) AS TotalSales
FROM Orders o
JOIN Products p ON o.ProductID = p.ProductID
GROUP BY p.Category;
```

This view can now be easily queried by business users to get up-to-date sales performance without needing to write complex SQL queries.

This final project ties all the concepts you've learned throughout the book into a cohesive end-to-end data analysis workflow. By following this approach, you can:

- Collect, clean, and transform raw data.
- Perform in-depth analysis to answer key business questions.
- Generate actionable insights that inform strategic decision-making.

With this skill set, you are now equipped to apply SQL to solve real-world business problems, from sales and marketing to customer behavior and beyond. Whether you're analyzing sales data or evaluating marketing campaigns, SQL is a powerful tool for transforming raw data into meaningful insights.

www.ingramcontent.com/pod-product-compliance
Lightning Source LLC
LaVergne TN
LVHW022339060326
832902LV00022B/4140